black creole chronicles

Black Creole Chronicles: Poems.
Copyright © 2023 by Mona Lisa Saloy. All rights reserved.
ISBN: 978-1-60801-249-7.

Cover design by Alex Dimeff.

Library of Congress Cataloging-in-Publication Data

Names: Saloy, Mona Lisa, author.
Title: Black Creole chronicles : poems / Mona Lisa Saloy.
Description: First edition. | New Orleans, Louisiana : University of New
    Orleans Press, [2023]
Identifiers: LCCN 2023012228 | ISBN 9781608012497 (paperback ; acid-free
    paper)
Subjects: LCSH: Creoles--Poetry. | Black race--Poetry. | African
    Americans--Poetry. | New Orleans (La.)--Poetry. | Louisiana--Poetry. |
    BISAC: POETRY / American / African American & Black | POETRY / American
    / General | LCGFT: Poetry.
Classification: LCC PS3619.A439 B57 2023 | DDC 811/.6--dc23/eng/20230504
LC record available at https://lccn.loc.gov/2023012228

Printed in the United States of America on acid-free paper.
First edition.

UNIVERSITY OF NEW ORLEANS PRESS
2000 Lakeshore Drive
New Orleans, Louisiana 70148
unopress.org

black creole chronicles

poems

MONA LISA SALOY

Poems in this collection have appeared in the following publications:

"Black Creole Chronicle," "At the Whitney Plantation Museum" (original title), "Mrs. Bywater, My 2nd grade-school teacher" (original title), "Covid 19, 24 June 2020" (original title), "Pandemic Poem" (original title), "4 my Sister 2: Praise Song for Barbara Ann" (original title), "NOLA Post-Disaster 15 years 7 months," "Love," "#me too" (original title), and "God Was Willing Sis: I'm Home." *Persimmon Tree* 66 (2023): accessed March 28, 2023, https://persimmontree.org/.

"7th Ward Daily Fare: or Black Creole Talk," "Black Dudes with Gator Shoes" (original title) and "Resurrection Sunday: Tree Top Visits" (original title). *Obsidian: Literature & the Arts in the African Diaspora* 47, no. 2 (2021): accessed March 28, 2023, https://obsidianlit.org/47-2-toc/.

"Coming of Age in BAM." *Africology: The Journal of Pan African Studies* 11, no. 6 (2018): accessed March 28, 2023, https://www.jpanafrican.org/docs/vol11no6/final-Kim-14-Saloy.pdf.

"Covid-19 Chronicles: This Day, 19 May 2020" (original title), *Konch Journal* 1 (2020): accessed March 27, 2023, https://ishmael-reed.squarespace.com/special-issue-volume-i.

"For My Sister 2" (original title) and "Throw me Something Mista" (original title), *Chicago Quarterly Review* 33 (2021): 219–220.

"God Was Willing Sis: I'm Home," *Poem-a-Day*, last modified Sept. 14, 2022, accessed Feb. 17, 2023, https://poets.org/ poem/god-was-willing-sis-im-home?mc_cid=0b1c8ce38d&mc_ei- d=78babb953a.

"Lincoln Beach," "For My Sister 2" (original title), and "From Bondage to Freedom" in *Black Gold, an Anthology of the Best Black Poetry in the Africa & African American World*, edited by Ja A. Jahannes (Savannah: Turner Mayfield Publishing, 2014), 219–226.

"Pandemic Poem 15 July 2020 as Bullets Fly" (original title) and "We Matter," *A Gathering of the Tribes* 16 (2022): 134.

"7th Ward Daily Fare" (original title), "Resurrection Sunday: Tree Top Visits" (original title), and "Years Ago Before the Storm" (original title) in *Black Fire This Time*, edited by Kim McMillon (Detroit: Aquarius Press, 2022), 424–428.

Thank you Almighty God for this life, my family, for my people.

For my people everywhere, united by culture, separated by seas.

Thanks Oh Lord, You've Taken Us to Here

Thank you Lord in Heaven
For all your Blessings
For all the trials that took us to here
We've ached too much
We've cried too much
We've lied too much
Almost died too much too often even in these days & times
Lord, bless the souls of those taken too soon too violently
    stolen
We've longed too much for all that is not good for us
We've laughed a lot even at the hard knocks felt each age
    Lord
We've inhaled too much trying dying finally beginning to
    breathe
We've devoured our dreams & spit them on steps to nowhere
We've seen too much hurt too much hunger too much pain
Not to know that we are not in charge that
By your Grace we stand having
Created culture & families & dreams of who we could &
    have become
We know
We thank you
We praise you
We honor you and
Pray those after us
Begin to understand just
How good you are to us.
Black Creoles say:
    By Grace, we're like good coffee,
    bad ain't got nothin' on our grounds.

—Mona Lisa Saloy

CONTENTS

Poetic Justice: Just Us

Hurricanes

Pandemic Chronicles: COVID from NOLA

Romance

We Matter

Poetic Justice:
Just Us

From Bondage to Freedom
Preamble

America, America
Rising King of the New World
Fueled & plagued by Trans-Atlantic-wide enslaving of
Blacks—Great Bantu from
Sierra Leone to South Africa
Sudanese from the continent's center
Atlantic to the belly of the Nile
Melodic Negroes
Black & brown
Egypt's allies
Great Lake tribes
Pygmies & Hottentots
Giant Kikuyu warriors, a
Pinch of Berber
Salt with Arab blood
Peppered in the West Indies, with
Gods & songs
Seasoned for two-and-a-half centuries
Cross with French, Spanish, Dutch
Portuguese, color Christian
Spice with East Indian

America, America
New World of a child's greed
Deaf to Black blues wails
Blind to the prison she made
Dumb to a morality empty as a new glass
America's conscience slept:

The Indians fought & died.
Negroes worked & multiplied.
It was a ragged world
America clothed in cotton
Negroes massed to millions
Like the cotton bales
Married to steam & water
Black labor spun a new America
Woven off Black backs with pyramids in their pupils
Transplanted Black bouillon
Built cities & commerce
Carried paradox & providence
Plantations & profit
Confederate hate
The Great White South
Canopy of heaven
Whose covenant
   The Negro is brick
   Our property our profit
   Our footstool our promise
   The Black gilt on our streets
Cotton kingdom
Few Negroes free
Some fugitives, thieves, vagabonds
Most were trapped people
   No family defenses, no free will
   A conscience chained like a child in the womb
   Chattel, real estate like
   A chair, a dog, or mule

So, in the bed America laid
Two sides: masters & enslaved Africans
Ignoring First Peoples
Free labor for profit
Black & white
Spiced with red Indigenous, a
New American South, an
Armed & commissioned camp
To stamp out slave revolts
   Gabriel in 1800
   NOLA Enslaved 1811
Vesey in 1822
   Nat Turner in 1831
   Crew of Amistad in 1839
   Black Creoles in 1841
Safety valve of slaves
Savior of the spirit
Determined dreams
Warmed in geography spelled on each heart
   Running away to freedom
Saved in song & story, a
Gift of human spirit & love
Sandwiched between right & wrong
America, the veil over truth
Slavery its unholy license, its
Black code a sham of law
America, bodyguard to tyranny mocking liberty
Cloaked in a hollow religious parade, & in the
Middle, the Negro
Savior & enemy of the new nation
Doomed to labor in those days spawning
Cotton, rice, sugar, indigo into gold

17

Shackled warriors
Witnessed the devil in Dixie, &
Bide their time

Black Creole Chronicle

Black New Orleans for true
Come Mondays
Some
Some will never see us
Some will never understand
Only some will get us, only
Some will dig our sound
Our joy
Our style
Our hip
Reverb our lingo our Tales
Tall & squat & old as the world
Will they see who or what she or he is or they are?

Our crime was being Black
Our salvation, faith and
African Ancestry replete with exuberant Arts
Adaptable like lizards
We weren't supposed to survive whole
Black Creoles say:
  Now you got the picture
  With the right pair of drawers on

Creolesboro guardians of the Creole groove
Creoles can't stay calm doin' nothin'. We
Make guitar or piano solos or
Wail *one potato two potato* at play, or make
Salad with eggs to kiss your Pappa
Don't much bother folks
Who wake up to sweet smells of

Cane syrup laced on *galait* pie
Pan-fried shortening bread
Who makes the best oyster stew?
Who shucks 'em best fast?
We be doin'
We be don'
We be don' us, but
We *don't mind waitin' to see the Lord.*

In the meantime, we tell kids, there's
Ancestors in our veins, we
Called to the battlefield of life
Turn stumbling blocks to skipping stones
Slip slap smile or frown
Stories turn our necks around
Hold someone's good in mind, and
Be safest in somebody's prayers. Now,
    That's between you & me & the gatepost. Now.
    That's between you & me & the gatepost: Ya heard me?

7th Ward Daily Fare: or Black Creole Talk

In the Crescent City
We live on the inside of good luck, the
Right side of Blessings
Past front steps & porches
We're a giving thanks & praying town
Contrary to popular opinion
There's more churches than bars!
Annually, we count the storms missing us
Laugh & thank YOU Lord for another safe season
And in the middle of smiles
We see each other and
Wish y'all well
Until we chew the fat on the *gallery* again
 Hey, he looks like Uncle Brother. . . .
Naw, he look like Jessie Hill[1]
 Who dat?
Mr. Ooh Poo Pah Doo his self!
 Awww, they did that dude bad—
 Buried in old Holt Cemetery
What?
 Potter's Field
No lie; that's Capoo
 Oh oh gotta step
 Need to find a stump to fit & rest my rump
 Chew some pecans later
Amen!

---

1 Jessie Hill (December 9, 1932–September 17, 1996), a Black American R&B and Louisiana blues singer and songwriter, best remembered for the classic song "Ooh Poo Pah Doo."

Aphra Africana

Born at home on the four-poster my dad bought for $1.25
    a week
Daddy delivered me with a midwife
Said he slapped my butt first
Kissed my cheeks only after Mother kissed my face

Black Creoles both: Daddy could pass & did
Mother deep chocolate
Creole: a culture NOT a color, but
Some LA colonials claim Creole since New World born
Blacks raped wholesale; no choice in the sinful matter
Reason for some light some dark
No brown paper bag needed
Black descendants of mixed-enslaved Africans are
Creole
Six-hundred-plus-year-old Portuguese term, so named to
    define us
Creole means part Black in most of the world
Africa is Mother/Fatherland to all

My Pappa, maternal grandfather, born enslaved in
Sumpter, Alabama, walked to New Orleans to be free
Pappa lived to 110, a Baptist minister
Signed with an X long before Brother Malcolm

My grandmother was Black Creole, part *Tchoupitoulas*
My African Ancestry is Yoruba, Mali, Congo: all o' that
Call me NeoAfrica

NOLA-born
Sista to the Mother/Fatherland to
All the world
Black Creole

What We Know Now
That Was Not Taught in School

Transatlantic slave trade began in the
1400s, when Portugal, & other European kingdoms,
Expanded overseas to Africa.
Portuguese kidnapped peoples from the
African West Coast
Took those enslaved Africans, on a
Journey between Africa & the Americas, called
The Middle Passage
Could take four to six weeks, the average
Lasted two or three months
Such storms still reign on the Atlantic

The White Lion, English privateer ship
Operated a Dutch letter of marque
Brought Africans to the English colony
Virginia in 1619, a
Year before the *Mayflower*'s arrival in New England
Late August, when
Twenty-to-thirty enslaved Africans landed at Point Comfort
Today's Fort Monroe in Hampton, Virginia
Aboard that English privateer ship *White Lion*
These Africans
Commodities traded in exchange for supplies, some
1.8 million Africans perished in the Middle Passage[2]

---

2   Citation from a Robin Roberts *Good Morning America* segment featuring Tara Roberts, a Black woman *National Geographic* explorer and storyteller who collaborates with Diving with a Purpose, an organization dedicated to finding and documenting sunken slave shipwrecks and preserving African diasporic history: https://www.youtube.com/watch?v=OOZVSFZdIcQ.

The last U.S. slave ship, the *Clotilda*, of Africans to America
1860 landed at the
Bottom of the Mobile River in Alabama, found in 2019.

American direct importation of enslaved Africans
Legally ended 1808,
One year post the British

On the mighty Mississippi
New Orleans, the Crescent City
Sold more enslaved Africans than
Any American city

Enslaved Africans built European wealth
No middle class prior to African enslavement
Enslaved Africans built the wealth of America
They & descendants of mixed enslaved Africans
The Portuguese called Creoles, Blacks who
Gave America Blues, Negro Spirituals grown into Gospel music
Such sacred & secular musical styles blended into Jazz
Fused into Soul music, or Rhythm & Blues, into Rock & Roll,
    into Rock
Into Rap, into Pop, still evolving

Out of a cruel & forced migration of stolen people
Enslaved Africans were taken back to Europe or
To the New World for labor & their skills, the
Triangle Slave Trade, it's called
Estimates of thirty-six thousand ships took over five million
    Africans to the New World[3]

---

3   Roberts, *Good Morning America*; see note 2.

Then, Africans returned to Europe with the white gold
Sugar, coffee, tobacco; plus rice—
Long-grain rice really is Uncle Ben's, from
Senegal, the Gambia. The shotgun house
West African Architecture, where
Families lived during planting or harvest time
Imported to the New World, a must in
Hot humid southern air. The
Shotgun home, hails throughout
The New World, the Caribbean, South America
The American South, a mainstay
More gifts came
Soul food is now haute cuisine

Plantation homes stand still by labor of
Africans from the Congo
Who knew which woods did not rot.
Celebrated iron work of Europe, New Orleans, the
Refining of iron smelting of Yoruba, their
Handiwork remains Art through the ages from the
Ancient Akan Kingdom
Endrinka symbols adorn French Quarter balconies, gates.
Each symbol a proverb, a story, a legacy. *Sankofa*, a
Bird looks back to go forward

Now, my Pappa born enslaved in Alabama,
Sumpter, now a county, walked to
New Orleans to be free
Heard that all my life
Lived to 110
Me, just a new tween
He, the oldest, me, & two cousins

Larry is months older, & Dwight six months younger
Left in his care all our early days
Pappa held court on the front porch of our
Shotgun double, & folks came from
Far just to listen. What a storyteller, a preacher who
Co-founded Mount Zion Baptist Church on
North Robertson Street, which drowned & did not return from
Post-Katrina flooding, where his picture hung for decades
I thought Pappa told good lies, a good
Jokester, preacher dude, but
He lived so long, knew what many folks didn't
In college studying African literature when I learned
Pappa's stories were West African Tales
Handed down by word-of-mouth
Face-to-face, generation-to-generation Folklore
Pappa knew generations of families & could
Tell relatives what happened to Buddy &
His gang or Hawkeye & his girls. He signed
His name with an X half a century before Brother Malcom
Which is how the Army *knew* he was too old
To join World War I; though well built, still strapping and
Strong, for someone illiterate, he just knew too much
Official Army record shows he had to be over fifty & not
Thirty, so they said no. Already a brickmaker, bricklayer
Cement finisher, skills he taught his sons, who became
Craftsmen laying sidewalks, courtyards, churches from the
Vieux Carré, Treme, 6th Ward through the 7th Ward
Corpus Christi, Epiphany School & Church, Saint Raymond

Living through jim crow teaches daily lessons of
Humility & indignity, overt cruelty unchecked
Lynchings, folks disappeared, later found in pieces, or a
Dragging-death murder of James Byrd Jr. in Jasper, Texas
Murders of Travon Martin, Breonna Taylor, forever
George Floyd
To the more micro aggressions, some
Light Black folks accused of passing for white joke? Black
    Jap? Bl-Asian?
Some called "oh, you're only half the N-word!"
Our days & Tales celebrate the joy we make together
There's snatches of life during jim crow, the devastation
Sustained cruelty causes
Decreases in Black American numbers since 1790:
From being over 19.3% to 12% now. Blacks still
Jailed quickly for less than whites & remain
Jailed or die there
We are not half but multi-
Human, beautifully Black
and a lot more fun fanning cultures to live well, only
Justice is still "just us" America, but
We are more & more and
Blossoming

Coming of Age in BAM[4]

Last of the jim crow generation
jim crow named for a minstrel show
White man in blackface show called
"Jumping Jim Crow" into
Black Codes, laws after the Civil War
After so-called Emancipation
How whites react to newfound Negro rights: legal
    separation of races
We planned attacks with Homer Plessy
NOLA Civil Rights v. Ferguson, a push to
Integrate public transportation, then elect
Some Blacks to Congress
Public Education for all a first

Ku Klux Klan rose with first national blockbuster film,
    racist D. W. Griffith's
Birth of a Nation, then people's protests
Bloody Summer, 1919
NAACP & Urban League fight, later
Emmett Till & Scottsborough Boys fuel our rage
Brown v. Board of Education
Ignites hope

A child in the separate jim crow 1950s
Colored-only restrooms, restaurants
Leftovers turned Soul Food Cuisine

---

4 Stands for Black Arts Movement, a movement of politically en-
gaged African American writers, poets, playwrights, visual artists, and
other creators that took place during the 1960s and 1970s, sparked by
the Black Power movement.

Great Colored Cafés, Juke Joints
Back of town Jazz blossomed, bound by
Colored-only water fountains
Get groceries at the rear or side window
Couldn't sit at public counters

No Colored electricians, plumbers, truck drivers; all illegal
Some like my Daddy passed for white to survive,
Some to infiltrate enemy plans
Backyard parties, suppers, Second Lines
We passed a good time together anyway

Us, culturally covered, cozy, & Colored

Fueled by World Black Consciousness Movement
David Walker, Marcus Garvey legacies alongside
Rise of machines
Folks fed by Marxist critiques of capitalism, abuses of
    labor, finally
WWII-Blacks in the Army, Navy, Marines, Air
Forces saving peace
jim crow still ugly once home
Colonial invasions continued from the
1949 Chinese Revolution to the
1959 Cuban Revolution, more
International Black Intellectuals:
Aimé Césaire, Franz Fanon, Martinique; Nicolás Guillén,
    Cuba;
Nelson Mandela, South Africa;
Ngugi Wa Thiong'o, Kenya

A teen of the 1960s
Civil Rights Act passed in 1963
Not enforced until the 1970s
Larry Neal & Leroi Jones make *Black Fire*
Our Christian names flew into African tongues
Abena, girl born on Tuesday
Kofi, boy born on Friday
1961, Amiri Baraka arrested at United Nations
Protesting murder of Patrice Lumumba, Congo
Independence movements in Congo, Egypt, Ghana,
    Nigeria, Guinea
SNCC (Student Non-Violent Coordinating Committee)
Detroit Red blasted into Malcolm X
Taught resistance *by any means necessary*, then fire-bombed
Touched by God into Minister El Hajj Malik el-Shabazz
Killed February 21, 1965, then
Stokely Carmichael re-stamps
Black Power slogan, 1966
Reviving Garvey

We divorced Colored, a Negro
Eyes-to-the-ground cower for
African Dashiki-wearing Gospel singing "Lift Every
    Voice" folks
Flaming Black became beautifully bold
Kinks, curls, afro puffs fanned like proud
Black flowers from red bean to black to brown to yellow,
    all Black
Our great past unveiled from Akan & Yoruba Kingdoms
    & proverbs to
Banneker designs of the United States capital city,
    Washington, DC

31

Always blazing trails
Always inventing, from the ironing board to traffic lights
    to the first working computer &
Blood plasma; thank you Dr. Charles Drew
Jazz bopped to a *Love Supreme;* "So What" Miles blew
R&B wailed
    Ahhhhhh anh
    Oohhhh ohhhhhhh, Ray Charles's sunshine
Soul birthed Rock & Roll to Rock and
Whites would never be the same
Our poetic voices explode like fireworks: AI, Bambara,
    Amiri Baraka, Brooks, Evans, Haki, Spellman, Giovanni,
    Henderson, Kaufman, Walker, Young, Reed, Redmond,
    Carolyn M. Rodgers
Black journals pop up times twenty
    We keep our Eyes on the Prize Oh Lord Oh Lord
    We keep our Eyes on the Prize Oh Lord[5]

---

5   Folk song as sung by Sweet Honey in the Rock and James Horner.
"Eyes on the Prize ('Hold On')." Sony Classical, 2000, Accessed March
27, 2023. https://open.spotify.com/track/5NAQOsPYm2N1p3SjVP-
k9Vj?si=4568cf831dd43fd.

BAM & Me

Like the Harlem Renaissance or the Beat Movement, the term Black Arts Movement is something we say in hindsight, a label to honor & dignify a legacy we recognize as significant in many lives & affecting generations. At the time, post Brown v. Board of Education in Topeka, Kansas, the painful integration of public schools, & the aching protests & sit-ins of the heinous jim crow era, we lost great heroes & heroines—Malcolm X, John Fitzgerald Kennedy, Martin Luther King, Bobby Kennedy—and Fannie Lou Hamer said it best that she was *sick & tired of being sick & tired*. She articulated what we all felt, what our ancestors lived in the indigo & cotton fields of the South, in the subways & street corners of the cold North, locked out, looked down upon, often hated, misunderstood, & few outside of us really cared. Thank God, some did. Something wonderful happened. The era of realizing the continuous push for Civil Rights was raging. Most importantly, we, once Negroes, then Colored People, became Black & beautiful.

It was somewhere between the Black Panther Movement calling us to arms, to defend ourselves, as Malcolm X said, *by any means necessary*, & the Black Muslims practicing cooperative economics. Amid our newfound consciousness that traditional "Church" was historically hypocritical too often. Later came the birth of Kwanzaa to offset our newly found ability to promote buying Black. Then, Don L. Lee became Haki Madhubti & told *Niggas that to be Black is to be very hot*. LeRoi Jones called out an "*SOS, calling All Black People / Calling All Black People,*"[6] & became Imamu Amiri Baraka. Nikki Giovanni reminded us that even though most of us grew up poor (a sociological term) that *All the while we were quite happy*–especially since we had no idea just what we were missing since there was so much we were not allowed to do, say, experience; what we did do, say, & experience was great cooking made from whatever white folks didn't want, later called Soul Food, & now the stuff of massive cookbooks, cooking shows, & chefs, the hottest cuisine in the world. We sang our hearts out in church, praising the Lord in Gospel riffs born in the Sorrow Songs & Middle Passage woes added to the Blues of work songs & chain gangs. These gems became Gospel music that toured the world raising money for Historically Black Colleges & Universities. We cooked up something new between the Blues-baring, soulful stirrings of Black angst married to European notation making Jazz, America's original classical music. Then, Soul music broke loose into Funk, then into Rock & Roll, later Rock, later Disco, until those street-corner heroic narratives of Shine & the Signifying Monkey left the sidewalk from toasting into another musical phenomenon & blossomed into Rap, full scale. Yeah, we made more than lemonade. Through it all, our poets & lyricists, from Langston Hughes to Curtis Mayfield, gave us hope *to move on up.*

---

6   Amiri Baraka, "SOS," in *The LeRoi Jones/Amiri Baraka Reader*, ed. William J. Harris, 2nd ed. (New York: Basic Books, 1999), 218.

Lincoln Beach

My sister took us little ones to
Lincoln Beach, the Negro beach on
Lake Pontchartrain's shore of three thousand mini-me
    kids laughing
Every city had one then: us
Catching the Galvez, then the Franklin Ave bus, next the
Little Woods bus connecting us to
Haynes Blvd at Lincoln Beach. Seemed
Like we went to another Parish!
No car
Daddy said busses work fine
Walking is good for the soul
He didn't want the debt or become chauffeur; instead, he'd
Rather have family over on Sundays for
Backyard get-togethers
Cracking oyster shells for
Poboys on French bread from Dixiana bakery or
Boiling crawfish till ruby red cayenne pepper hot, like the
Sun beaming blindly in summers

On the way to & home from Lincoln Beach
We sang Smokey Robinson or "Backwater Blues." We
    Slept
    Kissed the bus windows
    Ducked white folks' stares
    Squeezed into seats in the back during jim crow. We
    Packed lunches, a few *plarines,*
    Creole homemade candies for treats. We
    Walked my first sand on the man-made beach

Swam in the BIG pool, me, no bigger than the kitchen
    table
Jack-knifed off of the high dive! Then
We fell asleep like bricks once home

Lincoln Beach, our beach, now
Decayed & deserted like old jim crow laws, but
Standing barely, crippled since closed. Then we
Took our cash to Pontchartrain Beach, the
White beach park, also gone, now a technology
Center just off the University, the
Black side of the lake road still not as polished as the
Other side near the marina lined with yachts
Wouldn't notice if it weren't so. Now, some of our youth
Kill each other wholesale for sport, some fake fantasy, or
Dead Rapper's dream of guns & glory, & they
Take no peace in bus rides, only lust for
What they don't own, want, have only a hand out, *gimme* . . .
God help us, & may peace pour plenty

Years Ago: Two Weeks before Katrina

It was hotter & more humid than now, two weeks before
  Katrina hit
The ink was not dry yet on my PhD
My cousins Big D & ConCon, & more family gave me a
Knockdown dance-up backyard party
Cousins & colleagues came from far
Elder neighbors who loved me through the hardest days of
Research & elder care of my Daddy, through the
Crack epidemic fake care of step kids who left
Daddy drooling from the putrid red beans, poisoned by a
Layer of moldy slime swimming across the top of the big-
  black-iron pot I found in the
Filthy mice & rat-infested kitchen, with only a piece of
  roof dangling
Roaches flying from nest-to-nest like birds; my family
  remembered, that
Crackheads stole everything not nailed down
Didn't leave Daddy a pair of shoes. I
Had to draw around his feet on cardboard for sizing; the
Shoe store clerk wanted security to remove me
Until I stood my ground, & left with a tan pair of
  huaraches &
Slippers for Daddy. Doctors thought Daddy deaf &
  deteriorating from dementia, but
He just closed his ears & leaking eyes to the
  disappointment he saw in his step kids &
transient men who took over his home, his life with no
  hot running water, a broken
Toilet, the weeds growing through the bathroom floor
  from the dirt ground, four feet

Below the claw-foot cast-iron tub leaning through the
Broken floor boards rotten from neglect

(Took me two years in & out of court to get rid of those
   niggas.)

It was the filth & poor nutrition on top of it, that
   diminished this WWII Army Sergeant,
Master carpenter, into a man who babbled, slobbered,
   who forgot who he knew; *my*
Daddy, who used to dance with my mother & shuck
   oysters at our backyard parties
Growing up. Had no idea what I walked into, just rolled
   his three-hundred-pound body in
sheets to clean him & change bed linens until the shower
   was installed—*his first shower*
since his Army days, he sang; he was happy again & came
   back to himself fully for
years, returning to stand guard on the front porch & greet
   family & neighbors or what we
call do(or) popping, talk stuff about passersby. Even his
   doctors were shocked;
We all knew: it was **only God**, & a lot of prayers

My new college colleagues, friends, & professors-now-
   friends came & ate Busters'
Plarines[7] & Chef Drew's bananas-foster bread pudding[8]
   with us, & danced the Second

7   Buster's Candy: https://www.busterscandies.com/.
8   Chef Drew for one-of-a-kind Bananas Foster Bread Pudding:
www.MillerThymeCatering.com, Email: mtcatering_2000@yahoo.
com. 504-563-2000.

Line with us on to Duels Street & A.P. Tureaud Avenue,
   laughing faces in Tune to Levert's:
   I ain't much on Casanova.
   Me & Romero ain't never been friends
   Can't you see how much I really love ya
   Gonna say it you time & time again
   Ohhh Casanova. . . .

They thought my family was celebrating my degree.
My cousin Larry said this backyard bash took him
Back to our old parties, that everybody came for me, not
   for a wedding or a funeral
   Bebe, nobody got married & nobody died! he shouted.

They came for me, for watching me love Daddy back to
   health
Back to himself, back to our family
And *yes the PhD*, a family first
Bringing us all together the way we were all raised
Only God, we said. *Only God*

Cicadas sang through the evening, serenading the nights
   until stopped only days later
By Hurricane Katrina fanned across the gulf. That was *our*
   family's last time all
Together with long-time elders. Mush, our Jazz crooner,
   the fishnet making *Leons* &
Great-Gumbo *Cerres* no longer here. I told my family,
   maybe I'll write a novel about
Those hard days of waking up to a *strawberry* peering over the
African beads on my dresser, & Daddy with no shoes
I'll change the names to protect the guilty

It was hotter & more humid years ago, the
Last time our family was all together
When nobody died &
No one got married

I ain't much on Casanova.
Me & Romero ain't never been friends
Can't you see how much I really love ya
Gonna say it you time & time again
Ohhh Casanova. . . .

Resurrection Sunday, Tree Top Visits

Resurrection Sunday
After the Gospel Mass
At D's House in the Neighborhood, the
7th Ward
No party today just cousins
Thankful for good worship
Healthy hands to bake red fish
Sweet potatoes
Tossed green salad graced with purple onions sliced peppers
Sautéed broccoli cauliflower corn sliced to tender, when the
Doorbell brought a tall chocolate
Bent-over dude carrying a well-used duffle across his body
Water bottle sticking out

Ohhh, he said. *Remembers me?*
Not really, but Happy Easter
His grayed jeans saw better days, his head capped in a bent
Knit mostly black with red, green stripes small but vivid
   D home?
Yes
   You remember me? Tree Top?
   You'se the couzin-poet?"
I holler, *Y'all it's Tree Top!*

Now, standing above six feet,
Tree Top's smile on a milk-chocolate face
Framed by flying curly dreadlocks most days
His crown
Today, cuffed in a red-black-green & gold striped-knit cap
D shouts: *Tell him to come in!*

Tree eases into the kitchen
Family central, slouches on a
Stool. *Sorry to come like this,*
   Sudden like, but Momma's gone now,
   Was forced out the house and
   Need to get tight for Salvation Army, who
   Charge ten bucks a night now & no
   Days work this week.
D shocked, *ten bucks a night; that's rent!*
Tree said if he claimed crazy
He could get free vouchers
But he ain't crazy & some things a man just can't do
His Momma didn't raise him to tell that kinda lie for ten
   bucks
Now looking into his pride of manhood
His handsome chocolate shines through toothless

He was one of Mush's men
Mush, our D's father-in-law
Our family crooner, jazz-bass voice
   When autumn leaves start to fall . . .
His fresh greens from ground he dug
Collards to heal the earth, Creole tomatoes for flavor,
   meliton in season
Tree Top, his *padna,* caregiver for his Mom, across the
   street, end-of-day sharing Heavy tree removal, or
   barbequing on summer days, Gumbo on cold days,
   sharing a Brewsky to
Jazz, Blues, Gospel, R&B every day
Occasional old-school movies in the yard
Tree, like Mush, told me to
Keep my old Toyota truck, just take care of it;

Danced Roots Rock with me to Marley Reggae
Made every Mush Birthday party, crawfish boil
Spring Sunday suppers in the backyard
We were together
We were safe, hugs by Mush
& his buddies who helped change a tire, oil, or send us to the
Right mechanic if they couldn't fix it
Neighborhood warriors all

This Resurrection Sunday, Tree Top stopped by
Checked in, left with palms warmed
By buckets of food, love, & dollars favor[9]
Our eyes leaked together
He would not take a ride
Wanted to walk to the bus stop
Holding our gifts in his heart
His head higher, his walk lighter
His lips broad
His lashes dripping leaks from smiling eyes

---

9 Dollars favor: D gave him some bucks for help.

Mardi Gras 2018

King Zulu Brent D. Washington
Section leaders of drums, the
Southern University band, holds open contests where
    students pick leaders
Tramps to Zulu Kings & Queens
Acts of defiance
Parody of Rex & white Mardi Gras
Opposite of their formality
Big cigar & back derby
Parade through Black neighborhood streets stopping at
    fave bars
Witch Doctor: promises great weather
Zulu is Black Carnival!
Black Beaded & feathered Warriors in new
Masking suits *are* Black Carnival

1952 Louis Armstrong is King!
Formed on Perdido Street Uptown. Some
Social & Pleasure Clubs rejected dark-skinned
Projected Bafoonery, the
Zulu Social & Pleasure Club way, mockery
Exaggerated costumes, lots of
African animal prints, though the
NAACP felt such stereotypes denigrated Coloreds, so
Black bourgeois rejected them
Until Brown vs the Board of Education
Until *Ungawa, Black Power!*
Until the Black Power Movement
Until the Black Arts Movement
Until Black became beautiful
Until some Civil Rights

All on a Mardi Gras Day film by Royce Osborn shows
Tutti Montana
Tutti's grandfather, first of the original Creole Wild West
Spy Boy dances, chants
  Big Chief coming round the corna
Three blocks ahead, paving the way
Flag Boy one block ahead of Big Chief
Wild Man used to be a low rung, but he protects the Big
  Chief
Cloaked in beaded & feathered suits of up to two
  hundred pounds
Hundreds of cultural stories in uptown suits
Craftsman Tutti, iron worker, metal latherer
Downtown jewels & beads & can see
People parading waiting for him to come
Neighborhood Black Indians all want to be prettier than
  Tutti Montana

Social & Pleasure Clubs, Benevolent Clubs
"The Rose Bud"—Tutti
Alma Batiste, Lionel's Sis
Miriam Reed
Original Baby Dolls
Men crossdressing too
The Dirty Dozen
  Hey la mis zerb fais my cob
  de menso fais my cob
  hey la mis zerb
Hot *Callas*
Skull & Bones gangs
Skeleton
Al Morris Skull Chief

Frightening experience
Big head little head
Bloody bones
Skeleton heads
May find origin in Haiti
Loa Madame Brigitte-Barron Samedi[10]
Death, purple
Wake-up call
Enjoy life
U R next
Musical hearts from cradle to the grave
African rhythms—polyrhythms
African instruments
Accent beats of four—Donald Harrison
Without music no dancing
Indian Red—don't change it
Black Indians tell Stories, Rap
Chants, hollers
Black Native Indigenous bead with geometrical designs and
African beading tells a story
Al Johnson's "Carnival Time"
> *The green room is smokin' and*
> *Plaza's burnin' down*

Black Carnival was on Claiborne!!
Justice-green
Faith-gold
Power-purple
City of Ancient Ones

---

10   Baron Saturday in English. Loa is a Voudun Spirit, and each has
attributes, purposes. Baron Samedi wears a top hat, a black tuxedo, and
dark glasses. Madame Brigitte is his associate.

Gulf & Mississippi Seaport
Always international
Africans from Senegambia
April 30, 1803, Louisiana Purchase
Most Haitians came after that the
   French 1718 New Orleans
We made it all new to 2018 & then some
Our hearts warm as the sun

We Dance

For Greer Goff Mendy
of Tekrema Dance Company & LA Dancers

Dance tells our story
Dance passed on by
Word-of-mouth
Face-to-face
Age-to-age, like all our ways
We start on the
Right foot
Get into a groove
Give a whirl
We follow in
Ancestor Footsteps,
We dance!
Dancing, the
Poetry of arms, legs
Swirling spirts to melody

Dance
Embraces life
Celebrates a moment like nothing else
Paints our Cultures
Fans our flames of passion
Laughter & joy pours on to floors or
Seats holding wishes to move

We dance on sidewalk songs of
Call & response
Kids at play, clapping, passing hands,
Swaying or shaking hips to sassy Tales

Ronald McDonald, a biscuit
Ooooh foxy Mamma, a biscuit
Ice cream soda pop
Shimmy shimmy rock
Down down baby
Down down, don't let me go
Sweet sweet baby
I'll nevva let you go
Or as Philly teens stomp to
  On the roof, oh yeah,
  It's one hundred proof, oh yeah
  It's in my locker, oh yeah
  A fifth of vodka, oh yeah

Our Ancestors dance in
Swinging arms flapping
Like swan wings or
Spread like peacocks of
Blue calm or Blues to wail and
Hail Heaven in sacred praise

We dance a dirge
  If I walk in the pathway of duty
  If I work to the close of the day
  I shall see the great king in
  His glory,
  As I walk the last mile of the way[11]—to
Mourn our loved ones lost, then
Hold a rocking Homegoing, hailing in hymns

---

11 "The Last Mile of the Way," hymn by Oatman Johnson Jr. (1908),
my grandmother's favorite, and often heard at Homegoings for family
and friends.

Some glad morning
When this life is over
I'll fly away....[12]
Handkerchief flying
Second Line dance honoring that
Life well lived

We dance & swoon
Counter-clockwise like
West Africans circling a palm tree
All dressed in one fabric the
Whole family, eyes leaking
Mouths laughing, dancing, or to
Our Savior, we honor his walk of will on the
Road to Gethsemane, our
Easter Vigil, the *Easter Rock* roaming
Round a long table in honor of that
Last Supper of Christ, laid out in bright
Lanterns, symbols of the Apostles,
Dinner plates loaded in special
Crab cakes, or Jambalaya enough to
Feed all the Saints remembered as
Honoring this Feast of Salvation
Dancing dancing dancing all night
Slowing at Sunrise to
Praise this gift of grace for all in
Negro Spirituals like
    Oh David Oh Lord Oh Lord Oh Lord

---

12   Hymn written by Albert E. Brumley, published 1932 by Hartford
Music Company.

When we dance
We feel
We flow to the ebb & rhythm
Sway to the sound, the
Vibrating energy that
Music makes in melody that
Touches our hearts, our
Heads to swoon and
Hands on hips
Clapping slaps in time
Bodies to bend and
Glide or slide left, right
Swing to drumbeats
Tap our feet, toes
Smacking shoes to make music of
Their own, embracing air like claps

From folk dances of Gullah Geechees to
Swing dances from the 1920s to
Jazz & Rock & Roll to the
Cha cha cha of Calypso thrills to
Black line dances alongside of the
Come on of hey,
   I'll take you there, ohhhh ooh yeah
   I'll take you there. . . . with Staple Singers or
Electric Slide to
   Get down on it
   Get down on it from Kool & the Gang or

Shaking that thing
Doin da Butt
Doin da Butt
Sexy Sexy.... [13]
Or ranking the
Stanky Leg or waving the
Nae Nae togetha! or
Tootsie Rolling knees inside out! or
Wobble wobble wobble at a wedding!

Dance for freedom as
We sang, marched, danced
Heads raised to heaven
Lift every voice & sing
Til earth & Heaven ring
Ring with the harmonies of liberty... [14]
Hands waving in praise
Arms locked folk-to-folk with
Street signs or stomping picket lines
We shall overcome
We shall overcome...
Keep your eyes on the prize
Oh Lord oh Lord....

Dance is a prayer to
Life that tickles our bones
Love with music lasting a lifetime

---

13   Experience Unlimited. "Da Butt." EMI America, 1988, Accessed Feb. 22, 2023. https://open.spotify.com/track/1erQfISWXcY-iSsTEYSaNUe?si=08b6c40d4d5c42d1.
14   "Lift Every Voice & Sing," written by James Weldon Johnson and Jay Rasamond Johnson, 1900: the Black National Anthem.

Faith in feelings past, present & tomorrow
Eternal as sky, or water, or talk
Taking us on journeys of
Me amour or
Miriam Mekaba's
  Dance Dance
  Mo Dance
  Banana fanna fo Dance
  Fi Fi Mo ance
  Dance!

I don't give a flying fart that
Some TikTok stars kidnapped
Twerking!
Cheeky Black, Mother of Bounce
Knows best with
Pussy popping—twerking those
Twerkaholics NOLA style, or
Bubbles in Trinidad of twenty-nine versions
Big Freedia Knows Best
  Bounce Baby Bounce Baby
  Bounce Bounce Baby
Gave birth, & we
  Boogie on down
  Boogie on down
  On down with EWF (Earth, Wind, & Fire)[15]

---

15 "Let's Groove." Columbia, 1981, Accessed Feb. 22, 2023. https://
open.spotify.com/track/3koCCeSaVUyrRo3N2gHrd8?si=4b7bc8b-
7619c42c6.

We be cool
We so cool, we
Bebop to Jazz, & Jazz it up, on a
Dance floor, then bop bop bop
We Mambo or
Hip Hop from Swing to Rap
No squares dancing here, & when we
Breakdance, ain't no breaking our groove
We like it funky
We spin, gyrate, & like all our ways
Folks kidnap Black fun but we know
Black Dance is ours
Born from the Congo to the
Coast of our cultures, wed to the
New World & flying home again to our
Mother/Fatherland all ours
Day & all night
Black Dance

Yearning is melody
Earning is music felt
The tax is movement
Dividend is endless joy
Head & neck bobs to beats
Hearts glad to sway with song
Dance for fun
Dance & see beauty move
Dance for grief & lift a mood
Dry leaking eyes
Dance for love
Dance & breathe
Dancing bodies don't lie, we

Dance like nobody's watching, we
Dance like there's no tomorrow
Dance like rumors spread, you
  Heard it through the grapevine!
  Thank you Gladys Knight & the Pips
Our fortune tellers dance at the
Crystal Ball, our
Southern University Dancing Dolls
Dance for Jaguar games each year, our
Baby Dolls dance street parades for free
Fourteen sets of Sistas swaying in serenade, like our
Ghosts dance to SOUL music
Dance dance
You dance
I dance
We dance
We dance
We dance
Yeah we do
Baaaaaaabbbbby

New Orleans Today: Music R Us

In the 7th Ward
Could be a Tuesday
May be a Friday
Definitely on a Saturday night
Some Folks are toasty, home in the
First chilly winter in years, but the
Beat of drums ring a
Street parade seduction
Tubas pounce & the
Horns rally as laughter roars
Feet dance, fastened to the
Bellies of soulful beats
Hands clap for joy
Handkerchiefs fly in
Joyous fun flapping while
Each wrist snaps in time nearing midnight
No funeral
No house party, a
Street corner slapping
Neighbors with joy
No matter how tired
No matter how long a week
No tragedy to mourn, but these
Moments erupt to celebrate & smile, from the
Inside out
Thanks to the Blessing of
Black music in the
Souls of Black folks @
Bullet's Bar owned by *de*
Mayor of the 7th Ward

Not for politics, but
Everybody's place
Grab a cold one with
Barbeque or
Brisket or fresh catfish hot plate
& an armful of joy
Ear-to-ear
Might be Kermit Ruffins blowing, or
Who knows who else
Working men
Painters & bricklayers
Cable guys or gas guys
Garbage men
Workin' women
Workin' the men
Some secretaries
Some ladies of the night
Some public health folks
Some food ways folks
Come to joy this way
Riding melodies jumping inside
Bumping up the outside
No worries
No frets
Pop that thang
Slide that side
Sway those arms
Flap those hands
Ride sweet music, an air journey
Destination happiness that
Echoes ear to hear
Hand to foot

Music in us
Outside of us
Music are us

Some people in their homes
Tryin' to get their rest on
Winding down from chores
Built up from a whole week's work
Thank God for a day job
Thank God for a side hustle
Pourin' a little cement
House sitting for somebody
People caring for someone else in need
Too pooped to pop
and all in a sudden
Music grooves burst into air
Filling the neighborhood with
Joy for blocks, for
Free

#rawsome

#rawsome
Oysters on the half shell
Must be an *"R" month*
Peacemaker loaded
Chargrilled love
Boom-boom eats
In a perfect world, I
Can whistle like
Professor Longhair

At The Whitney Plantation Museum, Louisiana

At the Whitney, the
Fields of Angels
Tells all

Woodrow Nash, artist of Akron, Ohio
Creates seventy-one life-sized kids from photos
Replicas of enslaved kids who lived here
Sweet faces with no eyes to
Symbolize the hopelessness of being enslaved
My souvenir pendant tethers a little boy
John McDonald of Baton Rouge, Louisiana
   No, suh, Boss, I can't read & write; when I was brung up
   ef'n my boss man ketch me wit
   A pencil & paper, it was twenty-five lashes.
Federal writers project narratives
Here is their wall of honor, the
Indigo nation
Generations enslaved
Moussa, Arabic for Moses
Mandingo Nation
Born circa 1778
None know for sure when, from a
Warrior nation
Coacou, born on Wednesday
Mina Nation
Born circa 1769
None know for sure when, then
Men called bucks, their
Job: make babies, make more slaves

Enslaved work begins by ten
Death comes in ten years for many
No incentive to keep the enslaved alive, a so-called
Renewable resource
1452 Pope Nicholas V
Sanctions enslavement
Pope Nicholas V
Given 250 slaves as a gift
Papal Bull decrees:
Dark peoples of the world
Savages to be conquered—giving
Religious coverage for slavery for over six hundred years
All enslaved denied their native names, new last names at
    baptism
Required: raised as Catholic, yet
Rarely buried, mass graves here,
Here, some two hundred kids
Can't afford to carry enslaved from the field
2,209 enslaved infants born in St. John the Baptist Parish,
Perished prior to their second birthday
Put into earthen holes

Occasionally at the Catholic Church; here,
(Haydel owned eight plantations at his height of wealth)
Catholic sanctioning of Black enslavement was
Not repudiated
Not ended
Until 1992 by Pope John Paul II
Who then apologized in Africa

At the Whitney, the
Field of Angels, tells all
  The whip is the lash of God
Only those who endured can explain

No Cultural Genocide

Do not disown the Blues
Do not ignore the soul of sweet sounds
Echoing kingdoms of
Akan, Ashanti, Housa, Igbo, Yoruba
Stolen for centuries, echoes in
Chants
Moans
Screams
From field hollers
Into work songs at every American Port
More Blacks sold in New Orleans than any city in
    America
Enslaved Negroes had Sunday afternoons off in
Congo Square for dancing, drumming, savoring *calas*

Talk about a good feeling gone bad, *hunh?*
Blues all the livelong day
    Hunh hunh
    Hung hunh
Tote that barge lift that bail
    Hunh hunh
    Hunh hunh

Snap those elegant & worn fingers at
Days done by dusk
Wailing Blues earned, wildly worn-through
Denims & aprons
Worn knees, no manicured
Hand nails here, just a
Blues wail to

Free our Ancestral spirits for
Some musical release in melody
Moanin moanin moanin *annnnh annnnh annh*
Real smooth or ragged like an
Aching hand & heart, *hmf hmf hmf*
Broken into bits, a
Banner of Blues
Earned like crushed
Spirits resurrected by worksongs
Blues riffs liberating lives
Married to Euro musical notation into
Jazz Jazz Jazz

Deedee bob deedee bop bop bop
Don't disown yourself!

Black Dudes with Alligator Shoes

Black Dudes with alligator shoes
Move in slow motion
Cool invented for them
They don't walk
They glide
Don't speak
Head tips back, one eye slants
A state a nod a wink with any luck
Not a flashback of 1950s or 60s
He's a *PK* & Comp Professor, an
HBCU youngblood
Aiming uplift at young minds

This youngblood
Descendant of dapper brothers
Who bought stingy brims &
Tailored suits on Rampart Street
When it was lined in Black outfitters
DeLarose Brothers fine shoemakers

They might have washed dishes or
Trucks or trains by day but
Nights & church days
Dapper was their name
Clean-as-the-board-of-health
Their game, gentlemen

Black dudes with alligator shoes
Move in slow motion
Cool invented for them

They don't walk
They glide
Don't speak
Heads tip a nod, eyes slant
Cool, a state of mind

Corpus Christi with Ms. Ruth

Ms. Ruth, baptized at three weeks old, 1929, her
Dad Edward Zeno, Haitian heritage; her
Mom Lucy Cobette, Black Creole both
Originally, they worshiped at St. Peter Claver Parish
Mr. Zeno, his mom French
Had Negro slaves; Ms. Ruth—*Femme de couleur libre*—
Then married a Negro & her family disowned her

Neighbors before I was born, in old days
Ms. Ruth, honored to worship at the first 7th Ward
Black Catholic Church downriver, says
Parents told her they had a barrel, a
Big one for folks to contribute to build the church, and
They did, nickels by dimes, bake sales of biscuits & cakes
Used to have so many people in that Corpus Christi
    Black Catholic Church
People standing in aisles, pleased in pews all over
Chairs in rear, so many Negroes together for worship

Archdiocese decree, a second 7th Ward parish planned for
    Colored
Expanded to Epiphany Parish & elementary school
The border was Dorgenois Street, so folks *had* to belong
    to Epiphany
Archdiocese decree. Our block began
Epiphany Parish, & we went faithfully, able to
Walk to school with siblings, from
Kindergarten, first Communions to
Confirmations, getting grown now, to
Eighth grade graduation. Ms. Ruth felt divorced from

Grand Corpus Christi Church. After the move, I walked
Ms. Ruth's son beautiful son Michael to Epiphany school,
   until
I went to Xavier Prep for high school
Michael later lost to AIDS, our
Hearts parted like a zipper

Ruth led Corpus Christi May processions to the Blessed
   Mother
Strict Catholic all her days
Lessons for those who love the Lord
Venerate Blessed Mother Mary, Mother of Jesus
Confession still serious business
   You couldn't play, Ms. Ruth says:
   You had to sit down & pray.
Solemn worship

Soon after that *grande* post-K flooding, the little Corpus
   Christi,
Epiphany Church stands redbrick proud, but empty with
Stained glass paid with sacrifices of members

Epiphany still empty, but bought by
Sigma Tau Delta Sorority, great
Sisters who love the Arts & the people

We pray for their dream of a community center
Epiphany, the second Black Catholic Parish
No longer a little Corpus Christi church, a
Community place for them & all of us
Ms. Ruth Zeno Barnes, Black Catholic Sista
My neighbor

My friend
Gone to glory now
With me all my days

Mrs. Bywater, My Second Grade School Teacher

Mrs. Bywater's home, a single shotgun a
Few blocks away on
Law Street, across from
What used to be Eddie's Creole Café
Where Daddy could afford to treat
Us all to dinner out together
Ordering anything we wanted: a
Cup of good Gumbo, with a shrimp or
Oyster poboy & bread pudding for
Dessert, laced with brandy butter sauce

At Epiphany Catholic School, Mrs. B. was one of the few
Teachers not a Blessed Sacrament Nun, who then
Dressed in full black habit, a few mean & racist
Mrs. Bywater checked our uniforms
Reinforced the pride we must take in
Our little selves even at six or seven. Mrs.
Bywater swung around our
Desks in starched white camp shirts &
Khaki skirts some slim & shapely like a pear
Some flared, fanning widely
Her hair coifed like a
Chocolate Loretta Young or a
Home-girl Lena Horn, elegant
   Speak up, slowly. Let me hear your
   Story, tell your story.

In her class, we were somebody
Already learning that young
Ladies carry themselves with care and
Help each other with book bags or
Lunch or being lookout at the bathrooms with no doors, of
Cement building blocks for walls, grey & dark
Where toilets choked, so we heard monsters.
Mrs. B. had our brothers escort us to
Play tetherball or walk home
Laughing but ready for homework &
Reading prep to come.

Mrs. Bywater, because of you,
I am me, educating, documenting
Our beautiful Black culture
Celebrating you all your years, then at ninety-four, ninety-five,
    ninety-six
We all love you, now gone to glory

PraiseSong: Dr. Samuel DuBois Cook

Dr. Sam
Morehouse Man at fifteen
Classmate of MLK, a
PK, preacher's kid from
Griffin, Georgia
Family man, fifty years a husband, dad, granddad
Author, admin man, educator, political scientist,
Activist & public servant, taught at
Southern U, Atlanta U, U of IL, UCLA
Phi Beta Kappa Honors
United States Army man, Korean War vet, former
Ordained Deacon White Rock Baptist Church, Durham, NC, a
Host of honorary degrees
Presidents Carter & Clinton appointed him to national
  councils
Humanities & Holocaust Memorial
Morehouse Man of many firsts
First Black Prez Southern Political Science Association
First Black tenure-track faculty, Duke U
  Forty-third Morehouse Man to President a University
Not just any: Dillard University
Where he reigned twenty-two years

Initiated the Japanese Language Studies Program, an HBCU
  first
Saw racism & antisemitism, two sharp sides of a divisive sword.
Keenly sensing rifts between Blacks & Jews, he began the
Center for Black-Jewish Relations, another HBCU first, the
National Conference on Black-Jewish Relations
Believed that Blacks & Jews "shared a history of oppression &

Common enemies whose final goal is genocide"[16]
Both suffered holocausts: Blacks in enslavement
Jews under Nazis; both at the hands of the KKK.
Cook wrote that *when Blacks & Jews fight,*
God cries.
Classic Prez
With an old-school presidential stance
Broad shoulders straight
Eyes ahead to tomorrow

Dr. Cook equaled the excellence
Demanded, expected, delivered daily
Decency & character the prize
Faculty, staff, students
Stretched us all to think well, act right
Lessons of God & good
History of ideas & global understanding
Rigor of study, integrity of work well done, from
Academic achievements to floral arrangements
Decorum, dedication, respect our daily bread
No such thing as second-rate work or standards, often he said
"Black academic excellence is the key to liberation."[17]
Welcoming all people
Dillard then had the most diverse faculty in LA
He mentored us all
We measured up or moved on
Moral core our center

---

16   Cook, Samuel DuBois 1928–," Encyclopedia.com, accessed March 27, 2023, https://www.encyclopedia.com/education/news-wires-white-papers-and-books/cook-samuel-dubois-1928.
17   "Dr. Samuel Cook Chosen As Dillard U. President," *Jet*, April 11, 1974, 60.

Navigating challenge & change
Social justice & equality our goals

Dr. Cook supported the Montgomery bus boycott
Writing to Dr. King in March 1956:
"You have achieved that rare combination of social action
    & love."[18]

Dr. Sam, like he said of MLK, was as "committed to a
Life of the mind & spirit as to
Social reconstruction & redemption."[19]

Dr. Sam, Morehouse Man at fifteen
Classmate of MLK, a
PK, preacher's kid, a burden & gift
Cook grew into, from
Griffin, Georgia

Classic Prez, a balm to all of us
With an old-school presidential stance
Broad shoulders straight
Eyes ahead to tomorrow
    There is a balm in Gilead to make the wounded whole;
    There is a balm in Gilead to save the sin sick soul.[20]

18   Martin Luther King Jr., "From Samuel DuBois Cook" in *The Papers of Martin Luther King, Jr.*, ed. Clayborne Carson, Stewart Burns, Susan Carson, Peter Holloran, and Dana L. H. Powell, vol. 3, *Birth of a New Age, December 1955–December 1956* (Berkeley: University of California Press, 1997), 203–204.

19   "Cook to King, 13 October 1961." Martin Luther King, Jr. Papers, 1954–1968, Howard Gotlieb Archival Research Center, Boston University, Boston, Mass.

20   "Balm in Gilead," Negro Spiritual. President Cook's favorite hymn.

PraiseSong: On Nelson Mandela's Release from Prison

Like the echo of a bomb or headache, your twenty-seven
    years linger
A caged voice, the whisper slaves, prisoners
Unchain us, break injustice's back

Twenty-seven years roar like Arctic surf
Against ruins of Xosa & Zulu dynasties
Whose footprints still lead our spirits

Our fathers, mothers linked somewhere between Atlantic
    mist
& tears of blood, the millions of Black cargo, the
Millions of South African children suffering

Who met their future in the face of fear
Nkosi Sikelele Africa, a prayer for
Africa at home & abroad
What we become lies between today's truth
Tomorrow's hope
Yesterday's blisters
Enslavement, jim crow, apartheid
Twenty-seven years, a bar on the ladder of freedom

PraiseSong: Coach Eddie G. Robinson

His father, a sharecropper
His mother, a domestic worker
Native of East Feliciana Parish, he
Played football at McKinley High and
Earned a scholarship through
All-Black Leland College in Baker, LA
As star quarterback. The
Baptist minister coach
Reuben S. Turner, opened the playbook, a
Coaching clinic, & birthed
Robinson's jim-crow-era dream to
Be a college football coach

He worked in a feed mill for
Twenty-five cents an hour
Before the Louisiana Negro Normal
Industrial Institute—now
Grambling State University
Needed a football coach
1941. Coach Rob
Taught offensive & defensive
Mowed the football field,
Fixed sandwiches for road trips through
Towns with no Negro eateries
Taped players' sore joints, even
Wrote game stories for
Local newspapers. The
Elbow grease for victory began, their
First season a bust

After a 9-0 unbeaten second season
WWII called timeout. By
1945, Coach Rob was back
Enlisting rookies
Two running backs
Till their parents pulled
Them for picking time
Coach Rob packed the players
Bussed out to the Father's farm, & the
Team picked the cotton
Coach kept his running backs, & the
Legend leaned on
Paying the price

His American motto is
Success equals hard work
Willingness to win
Making his boys better men
Passing on the things
Our society holds dearest
Coach Rob is more than a
Good coach with a
Little luck: four-hundred-plus wins
Fifty-six seasons
Two hundred ex-Grambling Tigers to the NFL, a
Win-loss Legend
How possible?

Some players call him a
Master teacher, like
Harry Crosby, Tiger alum
Who says Coach Rob never hurried

Always explained why to handle a
Ball this way or that, the
Advantage of a flawless play

Sixty-two yard Tiger field goal-er
Larry Scrubbs (Honolulu '75) says
Coach taught as much about
Life as he did football

Coach Jerry Lloyd (Dillard University)
Says Coach Rob brushed shoulders with
Many greats, recalls his office of
Memorabilia, a picture with
President John Kennedy, yet he
Always takes time with everybody
Mostly, his players knew he cared about them. . . .
It's hard to count the
Guys influenced by Coach Rob,
How he rooster's 'em up every morning
Gets them to class, . . .
Teaches 'em to be men.

Another Grambling alum,
Anna Lee Oubre of Alexandria,
Says that Coach Rob is *just*
Like your house
He's home
Always there, a
Good foundation
Anna Lee says you *can't*
Get too little
Can't get too big

For Coach; he'll talk
To anybody, anytime
He's a gentle man in a
Rough man's world, in a
Man's sport, and
Gives time when time's needed

Coach Rob testifies often that
He is the American Dream
When he says America is the
Greatest country in the
World, he means it
Says he'd be lying if he said
Anything else. Says
He never won a football game
Didn't tackle anybody
Didn't block anybody
Just that Grambling's been
Good to him
Grambling gave him
Opportunities to show
What he could do

Senior defensive end DeCarlos
Holmes says Coach stresses
Winning the game of life . . .
One of the most overlooked
Attributes of Eddie Robinson

Coach still spit out records
Burger King commercials
USA Today highlights, a

Sports Illustrated cover, a
Tank (Paul) Younger, a
James Harris, a
Buck Buchanan, a
Doug Williams. But
Coach's greatest record for
More than half a century
He had one wife, &
One job, a man with
One nation, &
One station
He is an American
Story of hard knocks
Graduating from the university of
Discipline & rive
Blessed with genius &
Caring for every young
Black man in his path
Preparing them for the
Opportunity knocking in life
Always urging them to
Win another one for Grambling

From the son of a
Sharecropper & a domestic to the
408 wins, 56 Grambling seasons, the winningest coach in
College football, who sent more than 200 players to the
NFL, the AFL, the CFL,[21] who says

---

21   Coach Eddie G. Robinson "spent fifty-six years at Grambling
State University, from 1941–1997. He put together an incredible over-
all record of 408-15-15 and sent **more than two hundred** players to
the NFL, AFL and CFL. [. . .] He was inducted into the College

He never won a football game
Didn't tackle anybody
Didn't block anybody
He just became a hero &
Humble leader, a man
With one nation
& one station
Paying the price

Coach Rob's American Motto:
Success equals hard work
Willingness to win
Making his boys better me,
Passing on what
Our society holds
Dear
Coach Eddie G. Robinson

Football Hall of Fame in 1997 and has received more awards than any other coach in history." *Black College Football Hall of Fame*, accessed March 27, 2023, https://www.blackcollegefootballhof.org/inductees/eddie-robinson.

PraiseSong: Barbara Ann (4 My Sister 2)

Sometimes I call her BAP
Black American Princess
She the beautiful
Beating out Shirley Temple smiles at five
Attending Martinez Creole Preschool
Speaking French Spanish skipping first grade. She recalls
   the turn
When Daddy returned from WWII, a Sergeant, cook, poet
Hungry to hug his first girl
Sis asked Daddy, *Who are you?*
Threw her bread down on the gravel street in protest, and
Daddy fresh from seeing French kids eating rodents &
   begging for food
Demanded she pick up the bread & eat it
Aries horns rearing, she stood her in her pride, then
Daddy slapped her straight: *Don't waste food*
Because Mother sewed tropical seersucker suits by day, it was
Sis who walked me through girlhood, assuring me
I could keep swimming even
When jim crow refused me Olympic tryouts
Stuck with me as her audience, she doo-whopped with
   other 7th Ward Creole girls
Danced at home under blue-light backyard parties to Etta
   James, Fats Domino, or Bobby Blue Bland slow drags
   with handsome
Creole boys of every hue & height
Under Mother's watchful eyes. Sis carved sputniks out of
Halved oranges & toothpicks with cheese perfectly
   cube-cut at the ends
Daddy strung lights from fences for their fun after dark

In her prom photo
Sis is pretty as a young Dorothy Dandridge or Lena
    Horne and
Daddy afraid for her beauty
Still laid a heavy hand on her freedom
Summers to Smokey Robinson songs
We Negro kids swam in water shows like Esther Williams
Sis & I always centered in a heart made of the best
    swimmers in Hardin Park
Each year with glued sequins on our swim caps to grand
Applause from crowds around the city pool—
She the beauty
Me the athlete & book kid
Both of us inhale good books
Brain food for the senses & spirit
One day, she announced she was leaving
Marrying a tall drink of hurricane—handsome too
Cut his '55 Chevy into a sports car called Lizzy with
Painted black footprints the size of my fingertips on the
    side mirror
Out of Daddy's house for the West Coast
Left one jail for another
Once Mother died, & Daddy drowned his grief in booze,
    broads, drunken
Parties with strange men, there for the Jack, one peering
    into my bedroom once
Daddy's face fell flat into the *Courtboullion* dinner I left
    for him
Had to go & landed on my sister's doorstep with
One bag & a new coat I bought with savings from
Lifeguarding or selling pleat-and-tuck pillows
Hand sewn on Mother's Singer

Stuck between scared & the next day, I cleaned, cooked
   their dinners, cared for
My nephew, washed & ironed their clothes, being useful
   & avoiding a future
My sister set me up for interviews with Larry Gossett, the
   activist
Son of her postal co-worker friend Ms. Johnny; Sis
Made me go to college, so I went kicking & screaming,
   then I
Took to it like a catfish hugging river silt; by Grace, I did
   more. Through
Four degrees, her hubby chided,
   Negro, when you gonna get a real job?

All along the way, I sewed for big guys—Garfield Heard,
   Big "Foots" Bob Lanier
Bob McAdoo, Globe Trotters, boy bands—and Sis sent
   me love in boxes of beans
Peas, stockings, priceless presents. She said, *go ahead*
You do what I couldn't
Study

Once a PhD, brother-in-law tempered by fighting to stay
   in unions, to earn
Rightful pay for his journeyman sheet-metal skills, & me
   working for the R1, he
Shook his head; I did alright, he admitted out loud

My sister outlives the love of her life, survives cancer for
    the second time in over thirty
Years, has two new knees that holler in airport security
    checks, a grown son,
Sweet friends, & we Jazz Fest each year in the Crescent
    City

These days, I call her *Execu-Sis*, who fundraises for the
    Central District Senior Center
On a hill overlooking Lake Washington; she chairs their
    Board of Directors, escorts her
Elders to St. Therese Catholic Church for Sunday Mass,
    rides ferries in
Puget Sound with her multicultural book club of ladies,
    all sistas

Today, when the neighborhood owls call morning to light
Before the hum of interstate traffic rises, I have a
Dark cherry & soy smoothie, put on the decaf, with
Chicory of course, plan to play something smooth by
Gregory Porter like "Painted on Canvases"
One of our faves, &
Give thanks for sister love in my life

God Was Willing Sis: I'm Home

God was willing Sis. It
Took sixteen moves in
Fourteen-and-a-half years &
Twelve different addresses since Home drowned
In post-Katrina flooding, now
I'm Home
Rebuilt our little shotgun house
Daddy bought for $2,000
On the GI Bill post-
WWII in the 7th Ward
It was wide enough to love
Two families at a time, double
Long & wide like a bulldog
Stocky with a sturdy gait
Seemingly indestructible
With its turn-of-the century
Plaster & lath between walls
Held by red-brick fireplaces
Anchors for kin to hold on to
Steady, outlasting many storms
From Betsy to Camille, hurricanes that came and
Went like occasional visitors who
Overstay their welcome
Here, we all saved every book we ever had from
Old Bibles listing births, marriages,
Deaths, to *Sherlock Holm*es & *Harvard Classics*,
Two dictionaries
American Heritage &
Webster's, plus the
American People's Encyclopedia, that

Answered questions
Daddy or Mother
Couldn't from newspapers:
The States Item, but especially
The Louisiana Weekly
Where Negroes had starring roles as newly married or
Debuted or swimmers
Medaled in photos with their
Part-time coaches who were
Full-time teachers like Vic Vavassaur, with their own
Kids too, who spent their summers
Saturdays & after-school time
Teaching us regulation sports from
Baseball, football, swimming to
Supervised play, where
We were all a team, & neighbors &
Grudges never lasted more than an hour or
No longer than a busted
Lip that's gone when the swelling fades and
Heals like our sunburns and
Summers between thundershowers
We see coming blocks away
Our shotgun castle
Our guardian of refuge from those
jim crow days in our
7th Ward neighborhood
When we had all we needed for
Comfort & summer fun of
Shaved ice or hucklebucks, &
Winters without cold &
No gunshots

7th Ward Tony

His Buddies called him Tony
Big Sis called him
Tony Baloney
Starched & pressed days
When guys dressed for gym class
His gym shorts of stiff lines
Pressed, & creased—he jumped high
Early on, like many 7th Ward boys
Tony was an altar boy by seven or eight for Catholic Mass, the
Devil hadn't gotten hold of him yet
For baseball games, everyone
Proud to don uniforms, his shirt & pants
Creased like a board, he ran hard
Caught fast balls without fail
His Coach, Mr. Eli Penny
Steered Tony straight
High school years
Tony tossed a St. Augustine H.S. scholarship, St. Aug
Home of the Marching 100
Right around our 7th Ward block but
Boys only. When
Mother took him uptown to
Xavier University Prep
Tony saw all those skirts
Pretty girls giggling, & a
Football team, another scholarship
All costs paid except for lunch!
Took three buses to get uptown to
Xavier University Preparatory High School
His choice, their champion

Tony won All-City in baseball, as a
Catholic high school senior
  Ain't nobody dope as me
  I'm just so fresh & clean
  Love the way you stare at me
  I'm just so fresh & clean[22]
Swam hard too

My teen years, he
Shooed no-good Niggas away
Humph, *Not with his Lil Sis!*
He ran some away like a Lil Poppa
Said only the best boy for me

His teen years
He paid me twenty-five cents to press & crease
His white jeans & khakis, while he
Cooked the best pastries:
Galait, pan-fried shortening bread, cut in strips for easy
   dipping in fresh
Cane syrup from Domino Sugar trucks
Tony made *galait* wide & thick like a pizza pie, sliced for
   eggs, with
Bacon & strawberry jam for brunch, or an evening dessert
He made no mess just great
Galait or lemon cakes, sometimes chocolate, still
Clean, pressed, & creased.
  Ain't nobody dope as me
  I'm just so fresh & clean

---

22   Outkast. "So Fresh, So Clean." A&M Records, 2000, Accessed
Feb. 17, 2023. https://open.spotify.com/track/6glsMWIMIxQ4Bed-
zLqGVi4?si=418622b8b5154fcb.

Love the way you stare at me
I'm just so fresh & clean

One time, his early teen times,
Tony sat under the Hardin Park shelter house,
Shaded from hot sun & peering neighbors' eyes, he thought
Hanging with fast boys & smoking Mary Jane, the
Aroma seeping into humid air, impossible to hide
Between Ms. Anna of the sweet shop across the street and
Mr. Joe coaching, running behind little kids
Mother heard before he landed home. Once, WWII Sergeant
Daddy arrived, smelled MJ on him as he passed
That leather strap kept only for bad beatings
Came out like a sneeze, & Daddy waylaid
Tony's butt black & blue, tears running down his
Face like rivers, no screams just moans &
Grimaces showed eyes crying, while
Daddy meant this 7th Ward Tony would not
End up a drug addict, like those lost men
Paid in heroin on the Mississippi instead of money
Daddy wanted Tony's tomorrows to tell a
Future of hard work, good skills, wholesome living
Tony's anger halted only when he slumped hard on the
Pine floor, weak from the leather strap now split in two
Afraid for him, my screams & cries so loud,
Daddy never beat him like that again
Tony never gave Daddy reason
Daddy's home, Daddy's Army-trained rules
Tony's eyes more solemn more grown, the
Boy gone
Growing into a young man

One time later that summer
Daddy & Mother argued in the kitchen
Tony didn't like it at all
Hurt Tony to hear Daddy fuss at Mother so
Ugly so cold so mean
Tony shouted at Daddy
 Stop talking to Mother like that
Daddy slapped Tony hard
I only cried
Tony stared Daddy up & down
Said calmly, a hard dare
 Do it again.
Wiping my eyes, afraid, then
No sound, no words, just stares
Mother hugs us
Daddy's anger melted

Our Dad, who built as a master carpenter, who could
Plumb like a plumber
Lay tiles or tighten electricals too loose, always
Starched, pressed, creased to start
Days of work
Daddy never missed a day's work from
Long years at the cigar factory to River Road deliveries to
Building wooden crates for new machinery at the
Port of Embarkation, Army Command Gulf
Closed mid-1950s, but Daddy would not leave NOLA,
 then to
Designing & constructing boxes for new ship propellers
Edward's Engineering, never lost one, even those
Ocean-going ones shipped to Australia

Our Mother could crochet, could sew
Aprons, or clothes covers, or ties, or dresses, or
Curtains sheer, or brocades to cover furniture, &
Cook the best Gumbo Sundays
Friday nights, when
Daddy worked
Days long as weeks, wearing indignities
Each hour each day; come quitting time, he drank at the
Corner Bar, the Fox, so sometimes
Mother took us on Mississippi River rides
Nights where we caught the Ferry, at the
End of Canal Street, riding the river like a
Cruise watching the *Vieux Carré* lights as
Tourists, for ten cents
Sometimes, only Tony & Mother went
Cruising the 'Sippi
Tony's time to tell Mother everything

Mother walked all over New Orleans to
Canal Street, saving bus fare for us, or
Walking to Dryades Street, the Negro shopping
Center when Jews gave Negroes credit for
Fabrics or kids' uniforms, or Daddy's khakis
Never sick always working at Haspel Brothers, so
We could attend Catholic school, or she
Played cards with neighbor ladies like
Mrs. Bradshaw, a hairdresser, then

When Mother could no longer leave the bed
Passed away in just a few months
Tony drove city trucks to spray for mosquitos
Like Byron Cerre, our friend, neighbor

Brother in baseball
Tony went to Flint-Goodridge Hospital to
See Mother one last time, but she was gone
Already being placed in a black body bag
They rolled Mother away, so quickly
Tony couldn't say goodbye
Crushed like all of us
Tony, watched, worked, learned
No Army for him
Left for Camp Pendleton, joined the
Marines, determined to one-up Daddy

Tony took his creased clothes to Marine Camp in
    California
Loved the Marine ethic: made Marksman/Expert
Always faithful, still
starched, pressed, creased
No wrinkles for him ever
    Ain't nobody dope as me
    I'm just so fresh & clean
    Love the way you stare at me
    I'm just so fresh & clean

Basic training, Tony made PFC
Boot camp champ awarded Cross Rifles pin early,
Once missing in action, my high school heart
Broke with worry & wonder
Wounded three times in Vietnam
Patched up once in Hawaii, resent to the frontlines
Served a proud *Semper Fi*
Won two Purple Hearts
Also anger, war's inheritance

One day shooting in forests for country
Vietnamese bodies falling like bowling balls
Next day, stateside
No decompression

Once done with Vietnam, Marine life,
Southern California, Compton life, Tony
Danced pro in night clubs—all kinds—for cash
Won club dance contests, easy money for
Swing, or Twist, or Jerk, or sexy moves
   Ain't nobody dope as me
   I'm just so fresh & clean
   Love the way you stare at me
   I'm just so fresh & clean

Tony, once AA degree trained, a construction project
   manager by trade
Ran building & energy plans for new western subdivisions
Founded Puget Sound Energy's Veterans Program to
Aid vets through crises, stop suicides, get better benefits
Daddy's son for true
Helped the Northwest Vietnam Veterans Memorial, even
Won Seattle's Leadership Tomorrow Award, always caring
   for all
Married, his third love & thirty-year wife came home to
Drawn-bubble baths, hot dinners waiting with a glass of
   her favorite vino
Tony later upgraded his dad-in-law's home

Great big brother
7th Ward Tony
Always there for me
Me with no place to live
Lost everything post-Katrina flooding
Tony sent needed bucks to help me afloat
Best big brother
Sweet hubby
Baseball buddy to many
7th Ward trained
   Ain't nobody dope as me
   I'm just so fresh & clean
   Love the way you stare at me
   I'm just so fresh & clean

Past many surgeries to fix his
War-damaged body
Now retired, he love golf for fun
Enjoy barbequing, still
Makes a good Gumbo
Clothes still pressed & pretty
   Ain't nobody dope as me
   I'm just so fresh & clean
   Love the way you stare at me
   I'm just so fresh & clean

7th Ward

7th Ward kisses the Mississippi where Esplanade begins &
Sashays her bottom at Lake Pontchartrain
7th Ward is home to Hucklebucks or Snowballs on a hot
   summer day
7th Ward is home to backyard parties of shucking oysters
   or sucking mudbugs
7th Ward life is Jazz, Blues, R&B groups like Chocolate
   Milk
7th Ward is home to Rouzan shotgun builders & Wanda
   who leads Second Line Bands & graces stages of Jazz
   Fest
7th Ward is home to Jelly Roll Morton & Sydney Bechet,
   original Jazz men
7th Ward is home to Jazz drummer Joe "You Talk Too
   Much" Jones
They say if you hear a 7th Ward drummer, he plays New
   Orleans
7th Ward is home to Baquet family Creole world-class
   Lil Dizzy's restaurant
   7th Ward is home to more Churches than bars from
   Beecher Memorial to Corpus
   Christi St. Raymond's Gospel Choir, Rock of Ages
   Baptist, United Fellowship
   Full Gospel plus
7th Ward is home to cooks' barbecue aromas that come
   with a taste across the fence
   7th Ward is home to neighborhood artisans the Yellow
   Pocahontas Group
   Fanning Beads & feathers of glory for over a century
   parading just for us for

Free or the

Hard Head Hunters & their annual *Cha Wa* Black
   Warrior parade, chanting, dancing
   Greeting Neighborhood Masking Men & us at Bullet's
   Sports Bar or
   Hardin Park

7ᵗʰ Ward is home to the historic Autocrat Club whose
   Friday fish plates
   Wednesday fundraisers help folks

7ᵗʰ Ward is home to sausage making Creole Bachemin &
   Vaucresson families—
   Theirs *tastes like more*

7ᵗʰ Ward is home to Social Aid & Pleasure Clubs, the
   Black Men of Labor, our heroes
   Who brought water to folks who fled flooding streets,
   then stuck safe in the post-
   Katrina Superdome before the National Guard came

7ᵗʰ Ward is home to the Circle Food Store since 1938
   across from Hunter's Field, once
   Ablaze with a Richard C. Thomas mural painted with
   thirty neighborhood kids &
   Little league baseball games

7ᵗʰ Ward, home to the "Spirit House" sculpture by John
   Scott, on St. Bernard & Gentilly

7ᵗʰ Ward is home to Valena C. Jones School & St.
   Augustine High of the Marching 100
   Who play for The Tournament of Roses Parade & a
   highlight of
   Mardi Gras Parades!

7ᵗʰ Ward is home to generations of families from Tureauds
   to Haydels from the musical
   Fitch clan to Allen Toussaint, who spent his last decades

near the Fairgrounds
7th Ward is home to kids blasting a trumpet on the walk
home from school
7th Ward folks greet you in the morning; or evenings, wave
from *gallery* or porch with a
Warm *Hey now!*
7th Ward is home

You Know You're in New Orleans

You know you're in New Orleans
Enter a restaurant and
Some melancholy Blues man
Wails
   Ohhhh Baby, Baby
   Ohhhh Baby
Aroma of fresh-boiled seafood hits your face to smile
Outside at the picture-window frame, a
Green lizard greets just
Bellowing that big under-chin sac to pink that
Fades before he scampers off into
Twelve feet of blooming iris
White & yellow blooms
Four Brothas shuck oysters non-stop
Keeping time to swinging hips of
Young brown women sliding into seats
It's Friday & Maze teases with *Before I let go* in silky
   sounds before I let go
Waiting for my hazel-eyed Soul Sista
Raised in Flint, bad water Michigan
Her B-day lunch today—she's late, blond & white but on
BST: Black Standard Time
Contractor call ring,
Tell him I'm eating crab claws, he
Orders a helicopter to me in his dream
Between big belly laughs
Teases a plea for a
Doggy bag of crab tails
Thunder claps
Rain pouring in sheets a block away

Skips us, dies at the
Causeway overpass. I'm
Flanked by Caucasians at each table
Two white guys, a dad & grown son inhale
Charbroiled oysters on half shells &
Seat dance
Carlton-of-*Fresh-Prince* style
Fists rock, they sway, laugh
Good food more fab than fear of
Black folks near
 Have mercy, Have mercy on me!
Food zones punctuated by good
R&B equalizing us all to
Enjoy first & last
Naturally N'awlins!

September Evening

Cicadas symphony at dusk, the
Waning golden light turns
Vanilla as Carlito's Mom yells
  Bébé, come inside now.
Sunday's last rest
Holding on to the weekend before
Monday screams us awake
  Thank God for a day job

The Revolution Is Televised

Permission: Spirit of Gil Scott Heron

When we were Colored, Negroes, & Niggers
Abused, killed wholesale, ignored
Taught to look down at ourselves, not into eyes of the
    privileged
Assaults were undercover
Lynchings rarely reported
Colored Sissies insulted, slapped, tortured
Young bloods disappeared
Some Sistas captured, killed, or raped, or
All of that
White Cops snuffed out lives
Families broken, busted, denied
Loved ones taken quickly
No witnesses dare say
No law in defense
Only tears & grief & loss left in those
Empty spaces

Gil Scott called out the
Revolution in hearts, mind, movements on
Each block,
Each family,
Each neighborhood
Where the revolution lives

Kudos to cell phone shots of George Floyd
    Body cams showing . . .
    Dash cams telling . . .

Six o'clock Blues now pans
Black Lives Matter murals on
DC streets, or George Floyd murals on
Sides of inner-city walls &
Monuments to such murders

The revolution is televised in
Amanda Gorman spoken word films
YouTube channels of Poets
Singing salvation songs and
Black Beauty uplift &
New mp3s on Spotify & in
Cultural Festivals around the globe
Celebrating Black Arts
Defying division & denial

The revolution is televised every day
Every way no need for
IncogNegroes or
Sissycognitoes or
Undercover Negroes of any kind

We be bold, new daily
Deliver ourselves climbing
Striving being

Now, the revolution
Is

Who Are We?

Beings, alive, blessed Black
Full of color, rainbow bold
Our story born in Africa Mother/Fatherland of all
Beginning of man & woman who
Left the sunbelt left Sahara hills left
Nile rivers left Kenyan mountains or
Gambian shores or Tanzanian islands
North to Europe East to China West to
India, Russia, to Pacific Islands or Mexico
Navigators of seas once *Gondwanaland*
Split into many lands, so Ancestors
Built Pyramids, the Sphinx, agriculture
Astronomy, astrology, medicine, Arts in
Bronze, gold, iron, masks of beads &
Woods that don't rot, Ancestors whose faces were
Glad & sad & regal, & made drums, &
Banjos, mbiras, & chants, moans
Hollers, with calls & responses, then
Colonial thieves came.
  The ax forgets. The tree remembers.
Our mighty kingdoms broken apart
Ancestors taken, shipped across the sea
Commodities, Black bodies
Packed like cigars, forced to breed, as
They stole fertile lands & enslaved our Ancestors, stripped
  of our tongues
Family, faith, stuffed unto Western ways
Made into beasts of burden & branded a

Problem, people to be ignored, or lynched, stomped into
   jails or killed wholesale by Police who protect & serve
   whites
   The ax forgets. The tree remembers.
Did we lynch whites?
Did we rape whites wholesale?
Did we starve whites? Did we chain them?
   The ax forgets. The tree remembers.
We jam on banjos, guitars, drums
We dance, sing, & shout the joy of
Black talk: *We be doin' it! We be jammin'!*
   The ax forgets. The tree remembers.
      If anybody asks
      Who we are?
      Tell 'em people of God!

Culture Juice

Take some
30,000,000 Africans from their Mother/Fatherland
Blend for 600 years in the New World
400 years in USA
Stir 300 years of bodies in chains on auction blocks
Rub tar & feathers
Cancel lynching & Colored-only johns
Spend 100 years in emancipation
Hopscotch around Black odes
Watch Ghana
Grate jim crow to integrate education
Plus 20 years of Civil Rights
Hello Africa
Add
4000 tons of elbow grease in the
America School of Hard Knocks
Sift
150 years of Blues with
5000 years of Sacred Songs praising God and
Lifting each other up in all our swag
Divinely guided
120 years of Jazz
(50 in the fields & back alleys)
75 years of Rhythm & Blues our
Soul Music with 20 years of Rock-a-Billy Rock
Weave Ska & Mento into that 4/4 One Drop
Reggae rhythms, *Passing it On*, Rasta style, then
Pour 60 years of Mothership Funkydelic Funk
200 of thin visibility loving our soulful strivings, plus
40 years of OG Rap

Love legacy
Leave respect for all Brothers & Sisters
Shake, rattle, & rock
Lift every face
From *café au lait* to chocolate
Thank our Creator
Toast today
Drink to tomorrow's triumphs

Hurricanes

Hurricane Poems Intro

Storms, a
Season
Mind prep
Supply prep
Leaving?
Staying? Then, the
Packing, the
Going, the
Angst, the
Arriving

Here are words of seasons past
Remembering humid heat, or
Fires burning our forests, from
Lightning strikes of hot summers, or in
Our hearts, or
Thundering storms
Kicking up the dust of disappointment
Living through it
Trying to live past it
That never happens
Disasters, personal, or
Natural disasters rather
Climate disasters now regular occurrences
Unavoidable as sneezing
Listening, seeing what unfolds, at least
My pen can tell the Tales. The
Good news is
Storms pass, &
We return to some semblance of normal

Until the next time. Such is life, a
Challenge at best; but as my elders always say:
 Every day is not promised, &
 What doesn't kill you makes you stronger. So
Get out the kitchen if the fire's too hot
Stew on that

We Remember Hurricane Katrina[23]

Only days later
TV news broadcasts that
The shock has worn off
Did they see the hollow eyes of
Folks moving zombie-like uncertain of
Any step in any direction
The shock does not wear off
The shock will not wear off
When a home is drowned or
Flattened by winds or
Burned by fire & every
Book, yearbooks, Bibles, Koran
Every bookcase, dictionary, cookbook
Every photo of family good times
Every fine plate
Every kid's award
Every piece of treasured painting
Every Blessed Mother statue
Every Crucifix, the one of a
Black Christ, a gift from your
Favorite cousin or nephew
Every suit every dress every shoe
Every hat every chair
Every table, the one you
Found at Goodwill and
Refinished by hand

---

23 Composed and presented for the Fifteenth Anniversary of Hurricane Katrina, a Poets & Writers virtual program curated and hosted by Kelly Harris DeBerry, Aug. 26, 2020, with Jose Torres Tama, Tom Piazza, Lolis Elie, Alison Pelegrin, and Asia Rainy.

Every carved African sculpture the
Mask of good spirits the
Aztec miniature totem from
Nwatel Chechhhuan
Every Mexican blanket
Every Ghanaian Kente-cloth scarf
Every vase broken
Every glass crushed
Every ceiling fan bent beyond repair
No place to sit or
Sleep or drink or
Wait & all the
Life
Lived there is
No more

Then, there is the block
The land now dead or
Swept of homes or
Burned to a crisp the
Charcoal film draped everywhere
No dads
No moms
No kids
No uncles
No aunts
No neighbors even the
Fussy ones
No dogs not a Chow or Shepherd or
Alley cat survived the quake or
Hurricane or fire
No gazebo stands

No porch shields
Not even a tree for shade
No begonia greets
No hydrangea laughs
No lily stands
When a neighborhood is
Wiped away
Only the hunger for
What *was*, when
Life was here

Summer Showers, Poem 4 August 24, 2020

Rainy season storm break
Cicadas announce late afternoon
Hear their symphony
Humming, rising
Like humidity after showers
Sweet surprises like a cool
Breeze in ninety-degree temperatures, a
Welcome peace between a
Lawnmower's roar

Summer showers fan like
Light laughter good for a
Minute or two of
Cooling off
Oh oh
Sun's still out!
Devil & his wife[24] are
Raising the roof off that
Hot spot of
Red & orange flames
Burning eternal
Trying so hard but
Failing to imitate
Heaven, even
Heaven on earth

---

24   During rains, when the sun shines, it is believed that the Devil is
beating his wife and she's kicking up a fuss.

Ohhhh Hurricane Ida

It was Ida who kicked all power
Electric & online
into the muddy Mississippi
A Category Four *Bi-atch*
Even leveled the AT&T tower—no cell service
Not even texting
What in the Gulf is this?
No hot water
Ninety-eight degrees in the shade made
Cold long showers better than key-lime pie dessert
Took Zoom meetings from my FJ Cruiser
Toyotas rock
Thankful I could drive to lines for
Ice, masks, power sometimes
More ice, & just to see where
Folks were—here, evacuated
Just me & a few neighbors?
Stubborn other folks in lines
Just like me
We smile, nod a wink
All thankful to pass up the
Gumbo flooding promised
Spicy sweat? We can hang in these semi-tropics
Live on our porches again
Pass the time with *Hey now*s as
Folks
Holler, *way y'at?*
Glad like me
Ida left us standing
Picking up patching up

Her ruckus
Ducking sunshine under *gallery* shade

NOLA Post-Disaster
Fifteen Years Seven Months

Early March breezy but bright blue sky
Sunlight touching every corner, sidewalk, front porch
Eastward wake up to soft tweets above sleepy heads
Little brown bird, fat bellied, no bigger than a
Sparrow, white-throated, a hermit rarely seen, bird songs
Serenade, a Thrush, a Finch, no matter but a mother
Seeking that spot under the roof eave, boards
Cracked in half, some fallen post-Katrina,
Repaired good as new three springs ago
When the whole family of Songbirds
Nested there inside from rain, winds, and
Carpenters hired to repair the long-empty
Hole marring the house front porch overhang
Meeting iron trellises on each side framing
The red iron bench, red-rust painted wooden doors

Mother sparrow returns each March seeking
Baby songbirds still nesting
Squeaking baby birds hungry seeking mother's
Treats of seeds, a worm maybe.
Songbird mom is like former neighbors
Visiting the empty lots between toothless blocks of
Homes missing, some still standing or rebuilt
They come in between *Mardi Gras* madness
Or before French Quarter Festival, the
Neighborhood noised only by lawnmowers
Kids batting balls at the park diamond or
Climbing the kaboom ladder trees with
Red & blue bars for hanging or curves for

Sliding, the neighbors nod a hey now, their
Heads low in memories of the spaces once
Filled with folks on their front porch, an elder or
Grandkids playing jacks or red light-green light on the
Sidewalk, all gone, even the house long
Demolished to a void of lawn
Like songbird Mom, they will never
Forget the smiling faces sucking
Crawfish heads in spicy joy
Washing the porch of seafood smells with lye
Neighbors look one more time,
By Grace they
 Keep on making a way, over & over again
 Keep on making a way[25]

25 Sample line from gospel song of The Brooklyn Tabernacle Choir entitled "Keep On Making A Way." New Haven Records, 2002, Accessed March 27, 2023. https://open.spotify.com/track/6vEGxE-EqE8uQClK6KgeEPz?si=9b0efaa580834f66.

Sixteenth Anniversary of Hurricane Katrina

In spite of Katrina, those here want to be here
Hollywood South again
Home to movies & television
Creole Cuisine an international phenomenon
Neighborhood Black Warriors[26] featured on
Treme, on HBO, still bead &
Await parade permits for after this Pandemic

Some elevated homes
Go more green, &
Black families still masking
Making music
Giving rocking worship services on Sunday mornings, if
  only virtually.
Blessed to escape shelters, relied on the
Generosity of friends & family
I've moved sixteen times, in
Fourteen-and-a-half years, had
Twelve different addresses
Lived in three states & five cities—and that is
Not uncommon.
Insurance companies stiffed us
Dropped us
No replacement monies like the other states
My family home, half-built for eight years is
Now completed, I am thankful
Home, as an educator, a full life of constant study, with the

---

26 Most commonly called Mardi Gras Indians, a nickname that
stuck, but each group has names, and they parade as Black American
Warriors fanning beauty for neighborhoods for free.

Rewards of grooming eager students for success; now,
    online amid a pandemic,
even more artists, elders, musicians gone, with the
    constant assault on our Black
men, women, youth. Civic responsibility, our
    neighborhood association work, is
gratifying & taxing; someone has to do it. I'm still
    stealing time to research, to
document Black Creole culture here, to write, while
    rebuilding my library one
book at a time. Sixteen years later, y'all is still singular
    & plural. The cicadas,
snakes, owls are singing again. Daily, I *give thanks* &
    enjoy reading a good book
or magazine on the galleries & welcome my family &
    friends
Home

Crescent City Rainbow

Not so humid August 10, two
Four-color Rainbow
Spread curly crescents across the
Horizon topping crepe myrtles,
Oak & magnificent magnolia trees
City Park, walking *le grande* lake
My daily 5K most weekdays
One year three months
Thirty pounds down walking
Today greeted by the first double rainbow
I can remember in so many years
Is it more rare with global warming? Or
Am I now outside more mornings
Coaxing my legs to follow my drive to
Reverse the clock of age, an a.m. walk. Then
Two rainbows fanned like sisters or
Brothers or the Canadian mallards in
Formation without touching just
Together magically trimmed blue
Yellow, red with a purple far-side edge
Only the third time in my lifetime, a
Double rainbow after days of
Flooding rains submerging sidewalks
Cars, lawns, steps, rainwaters, graves, water
Seeping into restaurants & living rooms now
Dry to today's gift of double rainbows
Joy: serious business
   Only God

Pandemic Chronicles: COVID from NOLA

Lockdown 2020

I.
Well, it's official
We marched into this
Everyone's on lockdown
Happy now?
Even the Irish had to cancel
St. Patrick's Day bashes
COVID-19 more deadly than the flu
Killing Black folks mostly, well
Welcome to America again
No time to be
IncogNegro
Folks formally too ashamed to admit they also do
Black talk among each other
Tweeting their fantasy future of
Blackity
Where we can just be our
Beautiful Black selves
Better wash your hands
Keep fingers out of your face
Cover your muzzles, eyes too, & well
Wash hands a long, long time
Then, singing all of the
Birthday song got old quickly, so I jam
While scrubbing with the Dixie Cups singing
Iko Iko
Iko Iko ande
Jocka mo fina
Annna nay
Jocka mo fina nay

Only, I sing the whole thing
Perfect for simple smiles & booty shakes
Maybe takes a bit longer
But happy all the while like Pharrell
Then by April, no Easter
Parade, no church baskets
No Church celebrations
April, indeed the cruelest month
Culture bearers not covered by anyone
No Black Indians masking on St. Joseph the Worker's Day
Hospitality workers out of luck
God bless them!
Free Wi-Fi that sucks.
Free movies we've all seen a dozen times
There's no restart to this Leap Year
Already years long it seems
Kids climbing kitchen walls & neighbor fences
ILon, six years old, tearing, says he's forgetting his classmates'
   names
My Big Rotty, Big Easy, wonders why I'm home so much
His sweet eyes speak:
   You again?
   What gives?
My new perfume is Hand Sanitizer #2020
They say the
Great plague or Black Death was from 1665–1666, the
Cholera epidemic from 1830 & by 1832 in U.S., the
Spanish Flu was one hundred years ago, a billion died; now
COVID-19 coronavirus: 2019–2020 in the world & the USA

Some cause for celebration:
Three Black writers win the Pulitzer Prize in literature:
Jericho Brown from Louisiana for *The Tradition*, poetry
Michael R. Jackson, *A Strange Loop*, drama
Colson Whitehead, *The Nickel Boys*, novel, plus
Ida B. Wells, one hundred years late, gets a special citation
   & $50k

II.
Ok, it's been some ninety-plus days
For washing accompaniment
I graduate to another NOLA standard, from The Meters
   They all asked for you
   They all asked for you
   The monkeys asked
   The tigers asked, and
   The elephant asked me too
While scrubbing dirt & cheeky virus
Residue down the drain
Gonna shake it all off
Shake my shoulders in time, with
June comes a cruel second for the
Shake up of sidewalk neck-choking, the
Lynching of another brother, so I
Celebrate in honor of George Floyd
Breonna Taylor, Alton Sterling, Tamir Rice
Michael Brown, Eric Garner
All those unnamed tragic deaths at the hands
Of racist cops hired "to protect & serve"
I'll sing my heart out
While I can, in case I'm next:

I'm gonna lay down my burdens
Down by the riverside
Down by the riverside[27]

---

27   "Down by the Riverside," Negro spiritual.

This Day, May 19, 2020

Home. Home only a year & four months
It took sixteen moves in fourteen-and-a-half years with
Tweleve different addresses since losing
Everything in post-Katrina flooding
Here in my 7th Ward Neighborhood
By mid-March admin said go home
Professors, students, staff. At first, I thought
This is a dream, must have
Heard them wrong, a fantasy, no, a virus
COVID-19 killing folks around the world
Spread like confetti at a
Mardi Gras parade, so go home
Stay home
Not the movie folks
Not the NBA, NFL, no Billboard folks

In just weeks, nurses, doctors, garbage men, grocery clerks
Are the stars—not the movie folks,
Not the NBA, NFL, no Billboard folks
Corona drama 2020. Then
Folks complained, forced out of work
Their freedoms denied but
Their lives saved
I'm not stuck at home
   I'm safe at home & after
Grading three hundred end-of-spring assignments
Final exams. I'm a
Blessed one, safely home
Can pay my bills for now
Read a book, binge-watch *Luke Cage* or

The Godfather of Harlem
Listen to Nat King Cole, Aretha, or H.E.R.
Can get the mail & groceries
Fight my fridge for control
Call my siblings & ask
Whatcha doing & really mean it
Call my cousins & ask
Whatcha cookin' now?
Call my brother & ask, *Did you read the one about all the*
People out of work?
All the people protesting to remove
Lockdown status & opening up the economy?
I feel their empty bank accounts & hurt chests &
Wonder what's to eat next
All I can see are all those people
Still alive to see another day like
Aunt Rose always said,
  Be grateful God woke you up this morning.

May 19, 2020

COVID-19: Halt on Homegoings
Elders always say
Every day is not promised
Today during COVID-19
We are reminded that a
Day is all we have that the next
Sunlight or thundershower
May bring a virus spray in just
Plain talk, they say it
Lasts eight-to-fourteen minutes in the
Air or fall onto a chair handle to stay
Days depending if wood or plastic or
Stone like even the head banner of those
Buried. Here, a funeral honors the
Dead one loved, who may even be
More hallowed in death, his or her
Right to have a proper Homegoing
To the Lord, a send-off that
Celebrates the loved one's life, and
It's not just the fancy casket holding the
Embalmed, dressed, presented body
At least one major reflection, a Eulogy
Provided by the families
Most are wordsmiths or storytellers or a
Neighbor who does that for those who can't, like
My dad who wrote many; now I
Compose them & read from a
Pulpit or for a wake, recalling not the birthdays but the brave
Who face lower pay, fewer
Chances to walk streets before accosted for

Being Black
Black men five times more likely to be
Killed by police than whites of the same age, ten times
More likely to be jailed for minor crimes; then, the burial
First a wake to visit family keeping
Watch with the newly dead, families so
Dazed with grief, they greet with tempered screams &
Grace holding them until after the loved one is laid to rest,
   after a
Church service laced with a Gospel-stirring service to
Comfort the sorrowful: at the
Burial in sacred ground, with pastoral Blessing,
Prayers of the faithful
Drenched in tears flowing long & wide as the
Family, friends, & neighbors attending.
Finally, the brass band buries the saint, then
Kicks up a Second Line blast of traditional
Jubilee songs:
   Going up yonder
   Going up yonder, to be with My Lord!

Not in mid-March
Not in April
Not yesterday
Not today
We can't send our loved ones
Home like we know how & love to
Thirty-six church members gone to C19
Fifteen former colleagues lost to C19
Too many greats taken by C19 like
Ms. Yvonne Bechet—highest-ranking female in NOPD still
Jazz greats: Edward Anderson PhD, trumpet man composer

Mr. Elis Marsalis, piano Jazz & Dad to
Jazz legacy sons:

Go long so.

In our hearts we still sing:

Some glad morning
I'll fly away
To a home in God's celestial shores
I'll fly away!

May 26, 2020

I.
Today, this day began with
Mother's Day sunshine, with a
Great horned owl's song, asking
Whoooo Whoooo Whooo? This month of
Virtual graduations, even the
Six o'clock news posts pictures of the
Newly graduated Blacks

II.
News reports more Black & brown
Dying from C19
The chain of hate continues
From enslavement to
jim crow to separate but unequal of
Course, no such equal sign met
Only tickets to ghettoes
To the back of the bus to the
Side windows of grocery stores to
Walking while Black
Babysitting while Black
Jogging while Black
Sitting in your own car, or
Sleeping while Black
God help us

June 24, 2020

Nadir says
No one is good
   Now
He's right
We can't breathe

Our necks bouncing off concrete
Like Alton Sterling
Like George Floyd

Our heads explode
Like twenty-year-old
Justin Howell
Who did nothing wrong or
Thirty-five-year-old
Jamel Floyd
Pepper sprayed
His asthma & diabetes
Screaming from mace
Sprayed to death
We cannot breathe like
Eric Garner's asthma
Squealed his last words
I
Can't
Breathe

We're afraid to be chased
Shot down like rabid dogs

Ask Ahmaud Arbery's spirit
Shot jogging while Black

Grief is too constant
Too long injustice
Just us
Too many Black faces
Litter daily obituary pages
No one is good
These days

July 1, 2020

Super spreaders
No symptoms
Higher viral road
They may talk louder
Sing out
Spraying COVID each breath
Go to a party or to a
Night club with friends
No social distancing
No physical distancing
No masks
All infected
All ill
Some more than others
Some no longer here

Freedom to breathe
Fake facts
Masks not necessary
President #45 doesn't wear masks
Trump's hoax
America is fine
Pandemic under control
Really?
Numbers rise by thousands
Hospitals near capacity again
More folks on respirators
More folks die daily

This American President #45
Does
Not
Care

July 8, 2020

Dried beans dried beans
Got a whole lotta people
On hold on lockdown still
Phase two
Infections rising like a new day sun
Spreading too fast too fast
We beat out Europe with rising cases
What's the prize? What's the prize?
More sick
More dead
This time even the young fall
Feeling invincible? Not on your life

Good moms & dads
Always taught their young kids
How hard is it to stay home?
Keep your distance?
Wear a mask?
Wash your hands good, real good?
Your life depends in it
Our lives depend on this—and yet
No calm
No patience
No boundaries
Folks out of control like
Bad kids
Who can't & don't
Listen
Listen

Mask up
Get Vaxxed
Do it
Or Die!

July 15, 2020 as Bullets Fly

Our 7th Ward is home
Where we know neighbors
Everybody says, *How're ya doin'?*
Ya Mamma & 'Nem alright? Alright?
   Yeah, ya right. We good BeyBey!
   Ya heard me?
G barbecues on his rear porch
Aroma fuels a bliss of smiles
Plus a taste across the fence
Some kids play tag in the street
Summer rights of passage heat or no heat, only rain will
   run them inside
One young mom sits in her son's baby pool, sky-blue
   plastic, enough to cool
Hot feet & a little boy who wants to see his classmates
   again
Rising 114 degrees in the shade & too many pandemic
   put-out-of-days' work
Waiters, bartenders, hotel cleaners, carwashers, grown
   men
Sit on corners, play tunk or poker under oak tree branches
Spread across the sidewalk;
Fireworks, fireworks, fireworks?
No: gunshots, gunshots more
Gunfire rings
Too close
Nine-year-old Devante Bryant shot
Dead at his home
God Bless his soul
Dad & Mom drowning in grief

7th Ward neighborhood in shock
Neighbors scared stupid
Teen gangs with guns kill kids
Oppression = violence
No safe spaces for kids @ home?
Not in our neighborhoods
Not in our homes
Not here
No
Not fair
Equality + Justice = Peace
America, do you hear the gunfire?

Father's Day, 2021

Forced pause
Think B.C.
Before Corona
What is legal kills:
Chokeholds
"No knock forced entry"
Armed police respond to a drunk
Sleeping it off
In his car, this
Drunk not driving, this
Drunk not killing via car this
Drunk in peaceful slumber

Why need cops pull
Guns for a drunk asleep?
    He's Black
Why force him awake agitated?
    He's Black
Why arrest a drunk asleep in
His own car not bothering anyone?
    He's Black
Only one week post-
George Floyd who
Couldn't breathe
Rayshard Brooks, twenty-seven, at a Wendy's
Tête-à-tête with cops for
Forty minutes before
Handcuffs come
He runs
Fearful, flailing

Fails to flee safely
Takes Taser, turns, fires,
Shot by a cop
Is shot, again, shot again
Modesto Reyes, a
Twenty-five-year-old welder
Killed by two shots in the back
  At least they grew up
Tamir Rice did not
Michael Brown did not
Stop killing us!

Feels like a time famine
Never enough time to
Faster phones
Faster computers, cars
Days, weeks whizzed by

Next normal
We choose to garden?
Write books
Play the piano
Read lots of books
Conscious moments
Recharge
Reset to human
Stop, see dogs laugh
Smell peonies
Pass good barbeque chicken
Over the fence still hot, the
Crack house burns down, only
Three residences left, run in the

Loudest generator in the south
Another fire waiting to happen
Like Ms. Velma says,
   When the dust settles,
   Let the rain wash it all out.

A Long Way Home

Last pandemic years
Took me took you
So far away to
Hospital views of those
Ill from COVID-19, the
Suffering of those who
Could not breathe without
Ventilators, & each time
We saw the struggling in
Beds raised or faces tubed
Our hearts went with each
Trial of strangers stuck in their
Houses, the kids bored or
Missing classmates or
Forgetting their friends' faces or the
News of Africans, or Asians, or Europeans,
Their ill numbers rising
Daily, weekly, monthly, their
Lovely cobblestone streets
Empty of people, like the many
Bars, eateries, shops empty here, in
Our hometowns
My brothers glad for wives & kids, and
My sister, my brothers, we could not
Visit; she with no FaceTime, & the
Guys with their wives giving those
He did that again? glances & laughing, then
Students started to read more & enjoy it
Think more, & listen more, and
We all listened to each other more

After a good or hard while, we learned that
We took a long way, many days, to
Be together, at home

Fall Day

Living oak tree tops fan under
Brown-grey squirrels slowed some but
Trapeze cable lines & evergreen leaves to
Peep through
Slim venetian blinds beige like the sky fading to
Dusk days post-Christmas, first forty degrees at holiday
   time in
Two years, what a shift of trust, from
Fake news like America First to truth of
Less dollars for education, health, care, seniors who
Paid in blood, sweat, & savings for decades but
Billions in tax breaks for corporations & wealthy

Christmas time of hope for humanity,
Mother Mary's message of resistance to stand for her
Faith in the future for all of us, reappear in
   #metoo #BlackLivesMatter #Christmas #love #give
#thankful #oldyearwans #bring2022better
#bless2day2orrow4all

Romance

Poem on Wednesday

It's not the small glass of
Dark red cabernet
Not the fact that I
Haven't had a beau in
Decades of working to rebuild after
Personal disasters of
Loss of home, neighborhood, to
Post-Katrina flooding to
Lack of federal response
It's none of that, but you, so
I text to see if you're up
Just to reach out to you
I reach for your voice
Your hugs with my face near
Your heart
I want to tell you nothing
Important as the weather, but
I find that I want you
Near me
Such wanting is new, the
Delight of a new flavor, the
Taste of ripe mango in season, and
Your manly shoulder
Leaning
Toward me

Love

On my birthday, he drove into my garage
This time, I had to open & close the door by hand, one
    huge push
Well, I was impressed
Once our eyes meet
We lean in
Kiss a sweet peck
He handed me a large beautiful bouquet of flowers, best
    of the summer season
Star-lily white, trimmed in purple over brighter white
    than possible by humans
Only God

It's my birthday
He was my high school sweetheart
What did we celebrate then?
A car accident concussion
Wiped so much of my life away
Disinfected the hurts & some happinesses
What were we like then together?
He a baseball wonder of promise
Me a swimmer retired by jim crow, with a
Grieving Dad drinking his sorrows
Each Friday, Saturday night at
Neighborhood bars The Fox or
Le Chat with night ladies swarming for his pay

Today, he brought me dinner
My fave: crab cakes from Landry's & Gumbo
He said he wished it was hot

The secret to reheating Gumbo I said,
Heat the rice separately then
Add hot Gumbo on top
Delighted—heated to perfection plus
Dessert: chocolate cake
This man feels like home, all
Divine, the
Best part
We listened to classic R&B
Frankie Beverly, we
Slow jammed to
The Spinners
Could it be I'm falling in love
Could it be I'm falling in love, ohh baby
With you with you with you[28]

---

28 "Could It Be I'm Falling in Love." Atlantic, 1973, Access March 27, 2023. https://open.spotify.com/track/5i0urffBRKl09GSX2Jhde-h?si=057792761b994396.

Valentine

All my life
Only my Dad
My brothers, & close cousins
Returned my affection, caring
Closeness, & companionship
Until now with you
No, it's not the giddy
High school crush we had
Or that spark of youthful attraction
That sets loins on fire
Instead, a grown affection, a
Closeness that feels like home
You feel like home to me
Thank you
For returning the caring I offer you, the
Loving moments &
Sweet clean heat between us plus
You are here for me as
Counsel, teaching me new skills
Handling contractors sharing
Great lawyers & as a
Friend who cuddles

It's a Happy Heart Day for me because
You give my heart a contentment
I've never known until you
Thank you for
Many loving moments; &
God willing,
Many more to come

My Dearest Sweetheart

God is soooo good!
I was alone but not lonely
Wasn't looking
For anything or anyone
Then you showed up
To listen & you did
To help me & you did
Only God
Then, we just kept talking
To each other
Sharing beliefs & goals
Then, a sweetness
Drew us closer with that first hug
My heart leapt for you. Only God
You give me such joy in just
Just being in your good company
Listening to your insights
I am learning so much from
Your wisdom
Your tenderness with me
Your loving touch
Teaches me to love you
How you enjoy
How you need to be loved
How you want to be loved
I am your willing student
Of caring, companionship, & comfort
Thank you for the bliss I feel
Thank you for waking up my spirit
Starving for you

I am learning that you bring
What was missing in my life
YOU
Only God brought you to me, the
Tenderness between us is a
Force for our good that I welcome
If you allow me
I am here for you & me
For adventures, romance,
Being our best with & for each other

Leap Day Disaster

He said he was working so hard
Traveling for work so much in
Shreveport for a week & a half
Baker, LA, one morning next or
Delacroix, then Slidell or somewhere else, but
He did respond to my texts of
Hug emojis & kisses from emoji lips then I
Message of what reports were done
What tips to tackle coronavirus or
Lenten meditations like
Let's eliminate negative thinking
Cheery good morning notes of
Wishing the best day ahead
Missing his voice
Missing our talks of
Working while we can, that
Age advances, & days ahead
May not allow legs to hold us well, or
Eyes to see so clearly and

He would finish at two o'clock today
Leap Day, an
Early evening of possibility
I thought, though he didn't say
He rarely does, which
I take as a tired man, no
I assume he wants to see me
I asked if we time was on his schedule
Yes of course he said, then
He didn't call

He didn't text
He didn't show

6:38 a.m., his text:
Want to have breakfast?
Hmmmnnnn, if soon I say
Worship Sunday, so okay and
We dine & dance around a
Saturday night missed appointment
My disappointment buried with a
Half hug & flying kiss
Such a succor I say and
Celebrate my Savior in song to
Ease emptiness & comfort caring

There's no fault in feeling deeply
There's room for priorities of
Time, attention, of joy
While here; but once gone, only
Dangers of dying by overwork
I warn
There's nothing attached to a hearse

You the Only One You Evva Gonna Be

You the only one you evva gonna be
Took three years to find myself
Was lost between a lost
Love & my self
Slipped away in the process
Like a snail scooting around avoiding
Salt, knowing it's bad
Erasing all sense of personhood
Avoiding my humanity
Losing touch
With the me I am
Reaching for anyone
Anything but me
Searching eyes
Someone anyone seemed, well, no
More forgetting who I am
I am the only me I'm evva gonna be
    Let the life I've lived, speak for me
    Let the work I've done, speak for me
    Let the service I've done, speak for me. [29]

---

29   Negro Spiritual.

For You

When end-of-summer heat
Holds well past ninety degrees after dark
Past a day of meetings on
Local Arts or reports of
Who came to college classes
After choir rehearsal
Teaches us altos the
Proper G notes to hold & when to
Stop, & sitting still
Is a Blessing—
Your message—a text—
You said you don't text but
You did, you said
Just to check in with me
Then your voice on the phone
That male vibrato breathing
A pause, when you take time
To hear about my day
Share your stretching
Stooping, saving property from
Pests from a spec to
Critters, crashing unwelcome,
Your voice
You there
For me
Thank you love

LA Jones, Good Brotha
R.I.P.

Oooooooo
Oooooooo
Didn't see him coming my way
Once distracted by suits &
Alphabet soup behind a name
There he was standing straight
Looking at me
Looking at me
All my hurt heart
My hope strained
Dampened by the crack epidemic
An invasion of poison to trust, history
Culture, family, stripping humanity from too many young
   & old
Sweet girls turned *strawberries* by
White-powder lies
There he was
Looking at me
Looking at me

My girlhood dreams of real love
Bloomed grown as hugs
Smiles just for me, his daughters,
Grands, my cousins, painting joy
Colors like a Gauguin sky blasting
Dawns blues & dusk sunsets of
Red-orange bursts blended
Gifts from God like him a
Help to those in need of lunch or

A Blues song old or new
Oooooo
Oooooo
Jay what? Crescent City soldier
Painting cultural crayon portraits
Black families together
Vieux Carré's St. Louis Cathedral
Fanned with Black Indian suits of
Beads gleaming,
Red, black, green feathers
Suits telling great Black stories in
Streets survived by Wild Men, Flag Boys,
Big Chiefs, Queen Mothers, all
Black Neighborhood Warriors

Good Brotha
Oooooooo
Oooooooo
Didn't see him coming my way
Distracted by suits &
Alphabet soup behind a name
There he was standing straight
Looking at me
Looking at me
All my heart hurt
My hope strained
My girlhood dreams of real love
Bloomed grown as hugs
Smiles kisses just for me & family

Even when his flying eyes sought
New turf, former loves, or whoever. . . .
He still cut my grass monthly until a
West Nile Mosquito bit his butt
Somewhere between the 6th or 7th Ward
Caught him into a coma, come fall, then
He woke to see me there in his room, his
Soul-singing daughter Troy
Called me there, said
I was the one he loved while flitting to other branches
Jones flew
To the Good Lord, smiling
Good Brotha
Good Brotha

We Matter

American Facts

No one wants to hear
How every other day a
Black man or woman or kid
Is killed by a white COP
The difference a video makes is
Racism in your face
Everyone saw some of them from
Eric Garner walking munching Twizzlers
Michael Brown Michael Brown
Silence is violence
No justice no peace
Global agreement denouncing
Racial injustice
In London, a once-a-week event
Blacks killed by cops
No chokeholds!
We can't breathe!
In America, two Black men a week killed by cops
In America, a young Black man is twenty-one times
More likely to be killed by police than a young white man.
Ask Eric Garner
Trayvon Martin
When do our kids go from cute to scary?
When will Black parents & families stop having to have
  "the talk" of
How to prepare for
Overt injustices, even being killed?
When will we breathe?
When will America tell the whole truth?
When will the USA be just?

When?
When?
Stop killing us!

Babysitting While Black

Babysitting while Black
A funny feeling called the cops
Some white lady alarmed
A Black man with two little kids in a car-rear seat
Police calls parents
Pulls car over
Gets kids out of the car
Concern why?
Barbecue Betty
Pool Patrol Paul
Now nosey neighbor follows
Concern for two white kids
He must be ...
He might ...
He's Black after all
  Catch him
      Jail him
          Stop him
Impossible he's a good guy
Just a babysitter
Some sinister escapade instead imagined where
Kids kidnapped
No escape
Why? Why? Why America?
Why can't America
Give a Brother a break
A pass a nod to normal no
No normal
Life for Black men
Forever the enemy

Forever the other
This time a Black cat
Bad guy
Automatic scare score
No reason
Only bad-mind fear
Fake concern
A holdback to power over Black people
White is right
Black is . . .

How to Disappear

Just about two decades
Post-millennium &
More decades
Post-Civil Rights
When Black became beautiful and
Africa, everyone's Mother/Fatherland
Post-jim crow
When Blacks were Colored or Negroes
Less than two years
Post-a Black presidency
Numbers don't lie, Black people
13.6% of America's population
Still mostly Southern
Where the sun shines and
Soul food is spicy cuisine
Beloved around the world, Black people
60% in ten southern states
2.2 million Black veterans from
Tuskegee Airmen to
GIs digging ditches in every war
When we serve, we breathe Uncle Sam
Blacks are
37.9% of prison inmates
Asian 1.5%
American Indigenous 2.2%
White 58.4%
229 Blacks blasted dead by Cops since
George Floyd
  Fix me Jesus Fix me
  Fix me Jesus Fix me

Erase Tyranny of Today

Historic New Orleans Collection Commission, Spring 2021

Yesterday cries ancestral blood, blood
Dripping from chains or lynchings
Black culture denied
Sisters torn from mother, father, brother
Centuries without a mother tongue or faith or
Knowledge of kingdoms
Too vast to name in our Mother/Fatherland

Our ancestors stolen, landing, forced into the New World
Their Tales sewn into brown skins
Sorrow songs echo with each heartbeat &
Eye blinking in time, in tune to memories fading but
    resurrected in each soul's food
Glad ways with each other. A New World now laced with
    a rainbow of colors, cultures
Made again. Even time & torture did not dim hope, often
    buried by the promise of
Politics, ideals of fairness, justice, for all, built on lies &
    broken ideals urging freedom
While formed on backs of brown skin ripped bloody, on
    stolen lands of *Indigenous*
Ancient *Peoples* devalued, dismissed, destroyed by force of
    church & law. Family
Language seizure, forbidden home customs, yet America
    born of hope in something
Better, a simple "We" for all the people; instead, bred men
    drunk on politics, not for the
People but power. His story every year, each decade, &
    century pledges justice for All,

paying forward for a few only, birthing systems of arrest
   & suffocation for anyone not
White, the stepping-stones of progress, wealth-paved

Truth matters
Principles matter
Our democratic ideal matters

Oppose Lies
Lies repeated again & again
Cannot replace truth. Lies
Do not erase truth
Half an angry nation
Riled by a lying
Liar-in-Chief
Losing outgoing President
Losing reelection
Losing fifty failed court appeals to
Overturn a fair, solid election
Lying again & again
Fostering fake news
Inciting angry *what-aboutism* on
More lies & more lies
Now impeached again

Anger addicts
Hysterical want-to-be patriots
Promote vandalism
Promote violence

Kissed by thieves
We count our teeth
Kissed by thieves
We count our teeth

Tell the truth
Vote the truth
Convict the guilty
Punish insurrection
Insurrection is treason

Let the Eagle vow to
Fan wings of freedom
Fly on the faith of
We the People
Heal this nation!
The people now fueled with
Faith & hope

Pride Apology Poem
for Cokie & all

To those of you still undercover
To those of you still wondering
To those of you proudly out
To those of you afraid of being outed
To those of you made to feel ashamed at
Any moment of your life
To those of you ever embarrassed by family
Ignorant of your right to
Live your life as you see fit
I apologize to you
I apologize for ignorance inflicted by & on each age like
    peach fuzz
Cloaked as hard-shell coconut skin, the
Arrogance of rotting
Teeth smiling through veneers
I am ashamed for them and
Me guilty of falling for great lies
Fear of the unknown
Painted as truth
Generations taught that "soft" men
Were punks or faggots or
Ginny women,[30] somehow cheap imitations
Missing the point
Missing the young man or woman, whose
Fragile life folds under the weight of
Fake bravado ignorant of the

---

30   Pronounced "jinny." Nickname for a non-homosexual male who seems to display personality characteristics typically associated with women.

Cruelty inflicted by each slur like
Butch or Dyke or Man-ish girl
Smashing confidence or
Feelings of the innocent
I am sorry for any such thought
Sorry for my first twenty-five years of darkness
Sorry for any hurtful opinion
Sorry for any verbal strike
Sorry for past ignorance
Sorry for any slight
For the years of hate bombing my brain
Bleeding into words not mine
Dripping like the mess it
Stirred onto any soul

You are whole whoever however you may be
You are more than worthy of life, love, pride
I pray you understand that
I did not know
Could not know until realizing that I, too
Am denied, dismissed, devalued by
Church, by his-story, by ignorance
Forgive me forgive me forgive me

I honor your life
I honor your choice
I am sorry for not knowing for
Playing a sick part in a sad game
Today, I celebrate you for all you are & will be
God bless you!

Pride Apology 2 U
for Cokie

After Katrina wiped me
Out of books, clothes, manuscripts, research, roof,
Shifting from coast-to-coast for work & learning to
   rebuild
Navigating architects, a series of builders, an
Engineer or two between moves from
Rentals in other cities then home to
NOLA again finally
When Ms. Zeleda agreed to rent
Me her upper room for cleaning, cooking, keeping her,
   but I said yes rent as well
Since I'd have to pay anywhere I stayed plus, I was
   working steady
Still Professor with summers off, & I'd cut the grass
Nurture her irises & roses even the potted plants; she was
   living alone, her kids
Grown with families & work of their own; I'd stop to chat
   with her, always holding court
On her lovely front porch framed in red brick & azaleas;
   she watched
Me care for my Dad & pass some time chatting of days
   when as a
Kid I helped her weed her garden when
Iris, her youngest, only wanted to play anything,
Long before Katrina winds passed, when all the levees
   broke drowning our beloved
Crescent City then coating Hardin Park in six rows of
   trailers ten deep, housing cops,

Firefighters, city workers, gone all day leaving unattended
    teens to run rough ways over
Empty & drowned homes like
Mine, so bored; daily, they broke the newly painted brick
    steps framing our perfectly
Paved cement porch that housed all our summer games of
    jacks, paddle ball, &
Hopscotch to an audience of siblings, cousins, neighbors.
    These kids with
No adult eyes on them breaking out window & door sills
    with no regard to the
Well crafted cypress doors or pine floors inside. There I
    was, landing in front of the
Lear home with all my worldly goods in my red Toyota 4
    Runner, & Ms. Zeleda's
Adult kids said *not here*. But I changed my address, had
    rent in my hands, there to help.
No

Officially homeless, I rolled my truck across the street to
    our gutted family double with
Broken steps & cried for the first time since the storm.

I called my Brother my Cousin D, who grew up here too,
    who hosted me & Big Sis
Each spring when we visited from Baton Rouge, my grad-
    school days of researching Kids lore following the Fitch
    kids, their friends, or capturing adult-male
Toasts from neighborhood Griots. I could barely speak
    describing my shock. D said *Come over here; you have
    people. Don't worry*

I could eat, rest, hunt for lodgings, thankful to be safe, welcome, another
Mouth in the kitchen but neither ConCon or D would take a dime from me

You, sweet Crooner of harmonies in the great tradition of Dad D & two grands Mush, a
Deep baritone swag like ("Autumn Leaves") (his Postman days) or Herbert Senior (bricklayer by day) who played stride piano, the whole keyboard while courting ears
With melodies, you were home for a visit, checking on family
We were all proud of all you did, holding on to every recap of recent gigs, then making
Wall art for a paint company & restoring plaster-architectural features, placing gold
Foil onto a historic capitol building, doing real good, making good bucks
Your arms now buffed to muscle, a grown man
Baring little resemblance to that almost narrow teen
Choreographing Perlita Street Kids performances for Jazz Fest, or the
Folklife Fest, or the six o'clock TV news crew
You always had rhythm, strong swag, a song in your spirit, but that
Large earring dangling
Shining against your face. Oh, we all
Embraced you with joy, glad to have you home, & me, oblivious to the grown you
Cracked, *What's with that big earring dude? Makes you look like a ginny woman!*

No matter my always-protective intent, no matter my
    ignorance of the
Newly grown you
When, the silence in the room slapped all talk shut, & I
    still had no clue until
You looked down to the floor, & our joy strangled by my
    stupidity: it
Hurts me still that my cheeky words cut your smile out
    even for a flash

I'm sorry. If I could
Take that moment back, I would

By the time you brought your handsome boyfriend home,
    & you two
So happy, & all of us happy for you both
Finally, hindsight taught me how cruel that moment

I'm so sorry. If I could
Take that moment back, I would

Words crush or build
Comfort or kill

I am sorry
If I could take that moment back, I would

Forgive me

Throw Me Somethin' Mista[31]

Throw me somethin' Mista
Throw me my pride in my step
Throw me my ancestors here, so we can *Cha Wa*[32] & chat
   'bout them, then & now
Throw me my Motha Mista, alive well before age fifty
   dancin' whole
Doin' dishes & trying to sing the Christmas song like
Nat King Cole *Chestnuts roasting on an open fire . . .*
Throw me into a good Penny Party[33] in the backyard
   Mista when
Chunks of watermelon on a stick cold makes me
Forget it was ninety-eight degrees in the shade
Throw me a tomorrow of equal humanity working
Together for a better life, a
Better planet, a better truth
Throw me into space Mista, the
Galaxy glowing glad on God's love
Picturing a peaceful earth from my left eye view
Throw me a penal system eclipsed of profit &
Promoting "rehabilitation" at the expense of voting rights,
   Mista
Throw me a new Constitution that eliminates the
   Electoral College now, whose need is
Outdated by technology; they don't vote with the people!
Throw me a real "for-true"
American Democracy
Where the people's vote counts

---

31   In New Orleans, parade goers' request for beads from float riders.
32   Cha Wa: Black Indian Street Parade in Neighborhoods.
33   Penny Party: a yard party where the entrance fee is by waist size.

Activism knows no age

I stand for those forgotten
I stand for those jailed for frivolous accusations, those
Sealed into life sentences for lightweight & often not-
    well-proven offenses
I stand for those dismissed by color, caste, lifestyle
I stand for youth without parents
I stand for girls NOT to be molested
I stand for elders trying to live well
I stand for schools without current textbooks, technology,
    or well trained educators
I stand for neighborhoods to remain safe
I stand for schools to remain safe for kids, teachers, staff,
    free from guns
I stand for stutterers, students with learning challenges,
    misunderstood by
Schools & anyone who thinks themselves better
I stand for honest, hard-working folks bullied by unfair
    people & work practices
I stand for women to get equal pay
I stand for ex-prisoners for the right to vote
I stand for an America for all of its people
I stand for neighborhood schools
I stand for Americans to learn the truth about its history
I stand for America to tell the truth about its history
I stand for justice
I stand for truth
I stand for peace
Stand with me!

#metoo

Violence is not always heard or guessed but
Whispered in shadow
Snuck around corners
Hidden under scarves &
Wrists of bruised bracelets or when
Pretending to be asleep and
Tickled awake, scared awake by
Unwanted fingers, mouths, &
   No one is safe
   No one escapes
Even the almost advances
The hint of I'll get you, the
Glares between stares of
I'll kill yo' mamma if you tell, or
Nobody'll believe you anyway, so
   If you see something
   Say something
   Tell somebody and
   Someone will listen
   May hear the fear in the
Throat that cracks
Between breaths of
Scared-silly calm, a cover
Like a hat on a bad-hair day
Scars under the skins are
Tender long after threats
Leave hearing range

If you see something
Say something
Tell somebody and
Someone will listen
May hear the fear

Once behind the dilapidated shed in the
Backyard, when all the kids played loud and
Ran around the poles for hanging clothes
Three boy cousins, boys over ten years old
Dragged me, their little five-year-old girl
Cuz with puffs of hair above each ear, their little
Cuz pushed to sit on the big
Galvanized tub used for crawfish or ice or crabs
It will be fun they said, but
  Take off your skirt
  Take off your panties
Laughing they said
I'm scared of a whipping but
More scared of not belonging
Pulled down my skirt
Pulled down panties
Exposed my little rear end to the
Air & mosquitoes & eyes of
Boys laughing their heads off
Taking turns slapping my little bottom
And me ashamed & crying and
Boy cousins coaxing me to pee and
I'm so afraid to move and
Tears streaming down my face and
Boy cousins laughing their heads off

Until a neighbor, mentally challenged Alton, hopped the fence
Grabbed the little me, pulling up my clothes
Slapped the boys to the ground
Before they knew what hit them and
Aunts, uncles, neighbors came running to
See my BIG neighbor carrying me crying snotty now
Under one arm & Alton
Dragging my two boy cousins by the collar with
His other hands long, fat, & wide like a fan
Not letting anyone go, then all the
Parents screaming since the neighbor was
Over thirty years old & mentally disabled, the
Aunts, uncles, neighbors thought he was going nuts
Between the screams of the boys and
I'm crying, a little five-year-old girl me & the
Babbling of a six-foot-tall man child, now
Screaming that the boys
   Made that
   Girl do nasty stuff nasty stuff was all
   He could shout *nasty stuff & they*
   Made her cry &
Me too scared to
Scream for help, so
He dropped them all at once after
All the aunts, uncles, & neighbors
Pulled at him from all sides for what seemed like an eternity
Making no headway & he holding on for
Justice for right for standing up for his
Little friend, me, who shares peppermints with him
Who gave him fudge I made for his birthday
Who sang his name in the mornings on the
Way to school & when coming home, *Heyyyy*

Al-ton! He saw something
He said something and
It was days before
All the aunts, uncles, & neighbors
Realized who was really at fault
Who really deserved a whipping?
Who needed to apologize & get punished, since
This was not kids' games, but pain poured at play?

No one is safe
No one escapes.
Every woman I know has a tale
This is mine.
   If you see something
   Say something
   Tell somebody and
   Someone will listen
   May hear the fear
   And help

Discrimination Poem #2

Blue Monday
Spring night spent in Bywater
The Art Deco bar echoed
"Ladies Night" "Ladies Night"
No cover
Drinks on the house for
Two hours
Any drinks

Bar maid & man
Pour for blondes first
Second
Third
Fourth my short
Afro kinky curly fluffed
Framing my more-than-olive face
I smile, watched for their nod but
Bar man & maid about-faced
Read the floor
Got beers for friends at the bar's elbow

They swiped drips of booze in
Puddles glistening in muted overhead
Bar lights softened for sweet talk

Hey Bartender, a drink here please?
  Wait your turn or leave, stern
Like I'd be sent to sit on the wall
Like a punished ten-year-old

Walked back to my table
Two moms two Poets
Glided out of tall double-wooden doors
Weathered shutters slap on one side
Bar man points to us a half-hearted
Fake plea to stay

We fly home, drained of
Momentary expletives: *what the f%*#?* such
Familiar disappointment showing on our faces, so
We smile, still happy together
Spring night spent in Bywater

Today, He Flew With the Spirit of America
For Jericho Brown

Today, he flew with the Spirit of America
This Tuesday after All Souls Day
After *Dia de los Muertos*
After All Saints Day
Left the Crescent City & a sparkling Mississippi & my
    chocolate city
Nouvelle Orleans, a place
Older than America
Caribbean North with Black Creoles from the
Bahamas, Barbados, Cuba, Honduras, Jamaica,
    Martinique, Puerto Rico, of course
Descendants of English, Chinese, French, Filipinos—
    (really just ask Lafcadio Hearn),
Germans, Italians, Irish, Mexicans newly come since
    Katrina, Scandinavians, Spanish,
Vietnamese too.

Well, it's just after lockdown
All of us still overshadowed by the boot on George
    Floyd's neck
JB flew first east to Ft. Lauderdale on Spirit Airlines
Airline of working folks
Why? Price baby, a way to & from
Lean unless you want extras like food, spirits, more
    legroom, etc.
See, the great hot living poet Jericho Brown tweeted
He flew too & was the *only* Black on the flight
Did I LOL? Yes, & he liked it; he really liked it
See, we, just academics, a studied crew of debaters of

191

Ideas & areas of inquiry. Mostly, we try to rise
Above the petty race cards
Carving new ground, but this day
JB can only be a Black man, who must
Be ready to navigate whatever
Folks throw his way

Jericho writes as a grandson of sharecroppers risen to
New York Times magazine covers &
Whiting & Pulitzer Prizes
He's brown, tall, brilliant
Others see only
His skin, though beautiful & brown, only
Fear rose that day, a reminder
How America hurts

Je suis Charlie[34]

Je suis Charlie
Je suis une Juive
Je suis une Créole Noire
Je suis Musulmane
Je suis une Américaine Noire
Je suis une personne complète
Je suis libre à dire la vérité
Aucune violence me taire
Place de la Nation Paris
Je suis Française
Je suis une Créole Noire
Je suis Charlie
Je suis Juive
Je suis une personne complète
Je suis le Monde
Nous sommes dans le Monde
Le Monde s'unit à Paris
Nous sommes une

---

34 For freedom of speech, *pour la liberté d'expression:* in honor of twelve staff members murdered at *Charlie Hebdo*, a satirical magazine in the 11th arrondissement of Paris, January 15, 2015.

Poem: What Racial Reckoning?

Watching George Floyd's last breath on TV by remote
    control is not enough!
22.5 years for Chauvin is not enough!
Who were enslaved for hundreds of years?
Who were denied family, education, worship?
Who are stopped more by police?
Who are handcuffed more by cops?
Who is jailed more?
Who are killed more by cops?
Who are hired less?
Whose voting applications are questioned more?
Rejected more?
Who waited last to vote?
Who are lynched more?

Who are fired more?
Who are educated less?
Who are ignored more for resources?
Who live in the worst areas?
Who have a harder time buying a home or land?
Who were enslaved for hundreds of years?
Who were denied family, worship, education?

Whose descendants received no reparations?
Where is the racial reckoning?

4 George Floyd

National crises
Racism cannot must not be normal
Eight minutes, forty-six seconds that knee
on Floyd's neck
Sudden death
Pressure on the upper back
No rollover
No sit
No stand
Officer arrested days later

Peaceful protestors
Glorifying violence, #45
Tweets: when
The looting starts, the shooting starts[35]

Kendrick Lamar singing from his heart on YouTube
   I just want to live
   God protect me
   I just want to live

I fight back with words on a page &
My knees no longer like my weight;
Words fight for me though, always

---

35   See Barbara Sprunt, "The History Behind 'When The Looting
Starts, the Shooting Starts,'" *NPR*, last modified May 29, 2020, https://
www.npr.org/2020/05/29/864818368/the-history-behind-when-the-
looting-starts-the-shooting-starts.

Words do not just have a cost
Words tell us right
Words tell us wrong
Words cut
Words seduce
Words trick
Words bruise
Words lead
Words lead right
Words lead
Wrong
Words crush
Words create
Words build belief
Words teach
Words tear trust
Words threaten
Words hurt
Words calm
Words soothe
Words heal
Words challenge
Words lift
If you be the shit
I'll be the shovel

Darnella Frazier filmed
Nine minutes, twenty-nine seconds, now the
World sees how badly Blacks fare
Floyd's autopsy
Homicide by asphyxia
No underlying health issues

What's his name?
George Floyd
Twenty-seven million bucks later and
George Floyd
We still can't breathe

We Matter

The past teaches us that it's not only big battles that count,
    but minor changes or events
May have powerful consequences, that literally chance &
    stupidity can change the
Course of history. Just look at Christopher Columbus
    who landed in the Americas
Looking for India. Adolph Hitler was a rising politician
    who became a dictator. America,
America, America, you promote a democratic ideal but
    govern by "representation"; you
Let the Electoral College go against the popular vote
    again. Where's the promise of the
Power of the individual vote, the rule of the people, the
    welcoming of the masses for the
Good of all?

My people my people
Some of us killed undercover
Some incarcerated for life or long terms for so little
Too many "allowed" to build on toxic waste dumps or in
    flood zones
Still we build our Arts from food ways to music from
    software shakin' butts dances

Well, refuse to languish in disappointment. Refuse to
    cower in fear of a super
Conservative political agenda for a select few. Let us
    recognize this mighty nation of
Immigrants as one of great potential & inestimable
    creativity. Let us continue civic

Engagement, public discourse, & creating literature that
  promotes truth not fake news
Or lies & more keenly recognizing misdirection.
  Encourage others to so the same, & do
what they can as well as they must to make this a better
  world of understanding,
Generosity, inclusion, healing, & earnest ethical endeavors

  This is our lives now, our future tomorrow. We cannot
  rest until we've given our
    All for a better America, a better world. We are
      responsible for this life, this
    Planet; & if this means that people unite around
      American mistakes still
    Exploding like confetti & blood & bodies, we must all
      do our parts. We are
    Not puppets but thinking, caring individuals who
      believe that hard work &
    Qualifications earned matter; we all matter. We, the
      people, will prevail

Imagine Freedom July 4, 2022

Happy Imagine Freedom Day!
Where folks can park or parade to
Celebrate holidays without fear of
Gunshots killing six people,
Like today,
Highland Park, Illinois
Bulldozing thirty others with
Wartime-like injuries
Twenty-one victims shot in Uvalde, Texas, at
Robb Elementary school. At least
Three hundred mass shootings this year by
Independence Day

Last night
Twenty-two smashed car windows in a
Downtown parking garage in
New Orleans; for one victim
His fourth smashed window incident

Where's the United States of America?
One Nation under God?
In God We Trust boasts
Our dollar bill
Instead a season of
Hurricanes in hearts
Anger. Akron, Ohio
Cruel killing
One more unarmed Black man
Twenty-five-year-old Jayland Walker
Shot sixty times

Ninety shots fired
Human bullet cushion
Such overkill of Blacks
Bloodthirst! Why do
Protectors shoot to kill? The
sweetness of neighborhoods
Disappear like seasons

Yesterday, another carjacking
Baby in the back seat, so the
Thief dumps the kid on the roadside
Thank God for the kind stranger who
Saw something moving
An injured animal? No
Someone, a baby
Looking for family to return

It's a damn shame. No, as
Ms. Ruth Zeno—daughter of a
Second-generation Haitian carpenter
Who built the first home on our block
Her big brother a Tuskegee Airman—says
It's a *sin & a shame*

Now, I can tell a
barrage of bullets
From fireworks and
I've never been to war
Danger zones are down the block or
Snipers shooting from interstate ramps

April 1, a bullet
Shot past my iMac
Missed my face by two inches
When I slid to
Rise for a pit stop, saw the
1.5 inch hole in my
Library/office window
That bullet sliced into my printer stand
Making confetti of envelopes
Only God

Thankful I'm still here
It's all our response—
Ability to work together for a
Better Africa, China, India
Help Ukraine, a
Better America
Less divided,
United
More free, a
Better
World for all

Glossary

7ᵗʰ Ward: My neighborhood. Wards are the original designed geographical demarcation of areas; *en français, arrondissement.*

Calas: "Calas are made of leftover rice mixed into a sugary egg batter, then deep fried and served dusted with confectioner's sugar. They're like beignets, only better—with a more interesting backstory," says Tooker, who hosts "Louisiana Eats" on NPR member station WWNO. "Calas was once a vital part of African-American livelihood in the New Orleans, and even helped some slaves there buy their freedom. [. . .] Scholars think slaves from rice-growing parts of Africa probably brought calas to Louisiana. Some trace calas to Ghana, others, to Liberia & Sierra Leone." (Maria Godoy, "Meet The Calas, A New Orleans Tradition That Helped Free Slaves," *NPR*, last modified Feb. 12, 2013, https://www.npr.org/sections/thesalt/2013/02/10/171663336/meet-the-calas-a-new-orleans-treat-that-helped-free-slaves.)

Capoo: Black Creole for bad luck.

Easter Rock: Ring-Shout Easter Vigil celebrated most notably in Winnsboro, Louisiana.

Galait: Pan-fried shortening bread made at home, before the general affordability of sliced bread.

Gallery: Familiar nickname for a porch.

Mayor of the 7ᵗʰ Ward: Nickname for the owner of Bullet's Bar, earned for his years of caring, contributing to block parties for Nights Out Against Crime, and fundraising for the Hardin Park Little Leagues. Immediately post-massive-Katrina flooding, he provided water, ice, and food cooked on the sidewalk for neighbors returning to view damage.

Meliton: Black Creole familiar term for mirliton, (chayote) squash, especially popular here in Louisiana around the holidays, often home grown.

Padna: Black Creole familiar term short for partner, a good buddy.

PFC: Private First Class.

Plarines: Black Creole familiar term for prawlines: sugar candy, sometimes made with coconut or pecans.

PraiseSong: While simply put, a PraiseSong is, according to Brittanica, "one of the most widely used poetic forms in Africa; a series of laudatory epithets applied to gods, men, animals, plants, and towns that capture the essence of the object being praised" (https://www.britannica.com/art/praise-song). My favorite definition is far more precise: "African names carry stories of who you are, where you're coming from, and what you've been through, so that you and others can 'know' you. If you were born an African child, you might be taught to recite a special chant of self-naming that identifies your family, community, and regional affiliations; proclaims your clan and revered ancestors; announces your place in society, as well as other special circumstances and characteristics. In a lifetime, an African person may acquire many 'praise names'—or epithets (= descriptive substitutes for a person's name)—which embody not only the virtues but also the vices of the person and/or the person's ancestors. So important is such African naming that sophisticated oral art forms called "praise poetry" have developed in almost every African traditional society." (From Cora Agatucci, professor of English, Central Oregon Community College, https://web.cocc.edu/cagatucci/classes/hum211/CoursePack/praisesongs.htm [accessed Feb. 17, 2023].)

"R" month: Literally, months with an "r," signaling it's safe to eat oysters on the half shell.

Strawberry: A person who trades sex acts for crack or other drugs due to addiction.

Tchoupitoulas: Louisiana Indigenous term meaning "people by the river," possibly derived from Choctaw.

Tramps: Carnival time costumed character mimicking early Vaudeville (Lew Bloom) or Charlie Chaplin's 1915 fare; a fan favorite of the Zulu Social Aid and Pleasure Club.

"Ungawa, Black Power!": Thrilling chant of the Black Panthers during the Black Power Movement.